EST
MOVEMENT AT RUTGERS

The Black Student Protest Movement at Rutgers

RICHARD P. MCCORMICK

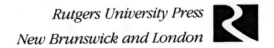

Rutgers University Press

New Brunswick and London

Copyright © 1990 by Rutgers, The State University
All Rights Reserved
Manufactured in the United States of America

Library of Congress Cataloging-in-Publication Data

McCormick, Richard Patrick, 1916–
    The black student protest movement at Rutgers / Richard P.
McCormick.
        p.   cm.
    Includes bibliographical references.
    ISBN 0-8135-1575-0
    1. Rutgers University—Students—History—20th century. 2. Afro-
American student movements—New Jersey—History—20th century.
3. College integration—New Jersey—History—20th century. 4. Afro-
American college students—New Jersey—Political activity—History—
20th century. I. Title.
    LD4756.M38 1990
378.1'981—dc20   90-30674
                                                       CIP

British Cataloging-in-Publication information available

CONTENTS

CONTENTS

Preface

*S*OME EXPLANATION OF how this account of the black student protest movement at Rutgers, the State University, came to be written is in order. In the academic year 1988–1989 the University commemorated the twentieth anniversary of that movement and of the inception of the New Jersey Educational Opportunity Fund. The project was called "Challenge '69: Retrospect and New Visions." It seemed to be desirable to understand what was being commemorated—to know what had actually happened in that memorable year—in order to establish the basis for the observance. I volunteered to provide a brief background paper.

As so often happens, the short report that I initially had in mind outgrew my expectations. It proved to be impossible to tell the story of what took place on the several campuses, supply a suitable context, and relate some of the consequences within the space of thirty pages. Even the extended narrative that I now present does less than full justice to the subject. But it may serve to memorialize the moment when Rutgers, like scores of other colleges and universities, responded to newly mobilized social forces by broadening access to educational opportunity.

To the extent that I have been able to recapture something of the intensity of those forces, I am indebted to the men and women who shared with me recollections of their own participation: Robert Curvin, Vicki Donaldson, Leon Green, Jerome C. Harris, Jr., Gustav Heningburg, Karen Predow-James, Charles A. Jurgenson, Herbert H. Kells, James Ramsay, and Richard Roper. The director of "Challenge '69," Dr. Eve R. Sachs, was unfailingly helpful, as were many others, including my colleagues, David Oshinsky and Richard L. McCormick.

Richard P. McCormick
University Professor
of History, Emeritus
December 1989

CHAPTER ONE

Introduction

S HORTLY BEFORE 6 A.M. ON MONDAY, February 24, 1969 members of the Black Organization of Students barricaded themselves in Conklin Hall, the main classroom building on the Newark campus of Rutgers University. They announced their determination to hold out until the University met their demands. These included measures for increasing the number of black students, faculty, and staff at the Newark units and for making the institution more congenial to African Americans. Their action was warmly supported by many black groups and roundly condemned by some political figures and segments of the white community. Racial tensions were high; Newark had been polarized by terrifying civil disorders in July 1967.

On Wednesday evening, there were demonstrations on the New Brunswick campuses. About fifty black students at Rutgers College (a men's school) and a slightly larger number at Douglass College (all women) entered their respective dining halls, filled their trays with food, dumped them on the floor, and departed. On the following day some thirty individuals, students and community activists, occupied the Campus Center at the Camden branch of Rutgers to secure attention for their grievances.

These dramatic actions had been orchestrated by the organizations of African American students on the several campuses to express their frustration with the unresponsiveness of Rutgers University to previous statements of their concerns. What was occurring at Rutgers reflected a national pattern. There were similar demonstrations on scores of campuses during the 1968–1969 academic year. Their common objective was to compel predominantly white institutions to change their policies and attitudes to accommodate to the needs of a multiracial society.

For African Americans, this meant not only broadening access to higher education; it meant as well the construction of an environment within which they could feel emotionally and physically secure and where their cultural values would be respected and legitimized. In the view of some participants, what was required was nothing short of a revolutionary restructuring of American higher education.

The black student movement that burst forth on white campuses in the mid-1960s represented more than an extension of the older civil rights movement.[1] In the early years of the decade, students from predominantly black colleges in the South, aided by some white allies, had waged heroic campaigns against historic racial barriers. Their methods were nonviolent and their thrust was integrationist. Their main targets were segregated facilities and violations of voting rights. By 1965, with the enactment of far-reaching legislation by the Johnson administration, they had achieved many of their goals.

Then new voices and new issues came to the fore. The attainment of civil rights had little impact on the plight of millions of blacks in urban ghettos. Their feelings of alienation and rage were vented in violent civil disorders—many called them

4

rebellions—in dozens of cities from Watts (Los Angeles) in 1965 to Boston, Cincinnati, Detroit, and Newark in 1967. Young black leaders now embraced doctrines that departed sharply from those that had shaped the civil rights movement. Poor people needed jobs, housing, medical care, and education, no less than civil rights. To secure these necessities, new strategies based on black unity, black pride, black culture, and, above all, black power were called for.

A new rhetoric was framed that drew heavily on the speeches and writings of such figures as Malcolm X, Stokeley Carmichael, Franz Fanon, Amiri Baraka, Eldridge Cleaver, H. Rap Brown, Ron Karenga, Huey P. Newton, and Bobby Seale. Often characterized as "black nationalism," the reshaped movement no longer sought white allies; neither was it committed to the doctrine of nonviolence nor to reliance on the judicial system to achieve its goals.

Black nationalist doctrines had a strong appeal to the students who were to lead the protest movement on college campuses in the late 1960s, especially those from urban environments. This is not to say that all black students, or their elders, shared the same views. But ideological diversity was often obscured by pressures for unity and by the symbols and messages that dominated discourse. Powerful images were created by Afros and dashikis, by chants of "Black Power" and "Close It Down," by raised clenched fists, as well as by boldly phrased "non-negotiable demands."

Militancy was by no means confined exclusively to black protesters. In the extraordinary campus ferment of those years, with highly vocal constituencies calling for an end to the Vietnam War, the banishment of ROTC, the abolition of parietal rules, for participatory democracy, sweeping curricular reform, and many other causes, militancy was the prevalent tone among many whites as well as blacks. University administrators and faculties found themselves quite suddenly in an unfamiliar and trying predicament; their authority was under attack and their traditional beliefs and structures were assaulted from many directions.

It is not surprising that the black protest movement targeted colleges and universities that had been predominantly white prior to the 1960s. Education was essential to empowerment. Outside of the South, where historically black colleges had long played an important role, white institutions had been at best indifferent to the aspirations of black youths for higher education. The tremendous demographic movement that shifted much of the black population from the rural South to the urban North after 1940 had been virtually ignored by educational planners. There was some recognition that elementary and secondary schools in the black ghettos left their graduates educationally disadvantaged, but down to the mid-1960s there was little disposition to confront the implications of this injustice. Meritocratic admission standards, measured by conventional means, were maintained.

Unfortunately, there is no comprehensive and reliable data on the number of black students enrolled in predominantly white colleges and universities prior to 1968. A rough estimate is that they made up no more than 2 percent of such enrollments in 1967, or 95,000 out of a total enrollment of nearly five million full-time undergraduates. Even the 2 percent estimate can be deceptive, for there is evidence to show that there was a *relatively* sharp rise in blacks enrolled in predominantly white institutions between 1965 and 1968. Federal legislation—conspicuously the Civil Rights Act of 1964 and the Higher Education Act of 1965—by prohibiting discrimination or segregation in higher education and by instituting a whole range of financial aid programs, spurred colleges and universities to take affirmative action to recruit and admit black students. On many campuses, their numbers doubled, and even tripled, between 1965 and 1968.[2]

Such was the case at Rutgers. In the fifteen years prior to 1967, only about two hundred blacks had received baccalaureate degrees, out of twenty-four thousand awarded. There were perhaps one hundred black undergraduates in 1965; by 1968 their number had grown to over four hundred, when they constituted about 3 percent of the undergraduate enrollment. Rutgers had graduated its first black, James Dickson Carr, in 1892. Over the next fifty years he was followed by no more than twenty others. Although the numbers increased slightly in the postwar years, it is doubtful that they approximated one percent of the student body before 1965. Rarely constituting more than a handful in any entering class, these students were highly qualified, unusually active in extracurricular activities, and destined for successful careers. They conformed, however uncomfortably, to prevailing values and did not overtly challenge the status quo.

On the eve of the black student protest movement, Rutgers University was in the throes of a dynamic period of expansion. Chartered in 1766, it had become the land-grant college of New Jersey in 1864. In 1945 Rutgers was designated the state university, although it did not fully assume that status until 1956. Then its management was vested in a Board of Governors on which state appointees were in the majority. Rapid growth followed. Full-time undergraduate enrollment soared from under seven thousand in 1958 to double that number in 1968. There were proportionately larger increases in graduate and professional enrollments. To accommodate this growth, the Board of Governors became deeply involved in managing a $200 million building program.[3]

The University had an unwieldly structure, which was to have an important bearing on its responses to student demands in 1969. Its main campus was in New Brunswick. Located there were Rutgers College and Douglass College (both of which were liberal arts colleges), along with colleges of agriculture and engineering and University College (the evening division), as well as graduate and professional schools. An additional unit, Livingston College, was scheduled to open in 1969 on the former site of Camp Kilmer, across the Raritan River from New Brunswick. On another campus in Newark were colleges of arts and sciences, pharmacy, and nursing, a school of law, and a graduate school of business administration. There was a third campus at Camden, containing a college of arts and sciences and a law school. The several undergraduate colleges possessed a large measure of autonomy and differing traditions, and each was to respond distinctively to the crisis that arose in 1969.

CHAPTER TWO

Stirrings of Change

*I*N SEPTEMBER 1963, the New Brunswick campus suddenly was made aware of the realities of the civil rights movement in the South. The March on Washington and the unforgettable "I Have a Dream" speech by the Rev. Dr. Martin Luther King, Jr., had already raised consciousness. So had the horrifying scenes of police violence against peaceful demonstrators in Southern communities shown on nightly television programs. Now those remote events were brought home by the news that a recent alumnus had been jailed in Georgia because of his work in behalf of voting rights.

Donald S. Harris graduated from Rutgers College in 1963. He went South to work for the Student Non-Violent Coordinating Committee (SNCC). Early in August he was in Americus, Georgia, conducting a voter registration drive at the Friendship Baptist Church. After the meeting had ended and the group had filed out of the church, police armed with guns and billy clubs charged the crowd. Harris was seized, mauled, and, together with two white coworkers from Harvard and

Trinity, was thrown into jail. There he was held without bail under a charge of "insurrection," an offense punishable by death in Georgia.[1]

Harris had been a well-known and respected undergraduate. Active in many campus organizations, he had played lacrosse and lightweight football and was a member of Phi Sigma Kappa fraternity. He was the founder and leader of Education in Action, a tutorial program for local schoolchildren, and belonged to the campus chapter of the NAACP. He had also participated in a Crossroads Africa program. With this background, Harris saw an opportunity for service with SNCC. "There was something burning inside of Don," his former roommate recalled.

Graphic stories about Harris's plight appeared in *Targum* in mid-September, accompanied by forceful editorials. Students, faculty, and administrators became aroused. *Targum* took the lead in establishing a Harris Defense Fund, which soon raised over $3,000. Addressing the fall convocation of the entire student body, President Mason W. Gross deplored the treatment of Harris and lent his support to the fund drive. At an evening rally that filled Voorhees Chapel on the Douglass campus to overflowing, a shocked audience heard one of Harris's SNCC colleagues, Charles Scherrod, describe the slayings and beatings that were terrorizing Southern blacks. A later meeting in the College Avenue Gym featured civil rights activist Bayard Rustin as the principal speaker. James Farmer, head of the Congress of Racial Equality (CORE) also spoke on campus in behalf of Harris. Senators Clifford P. Case and Harrison Williams brought his plight to the attention of the United States Senate.

Harris's supporters were instrumental in mobilizing more than three thousand persons, including black and white Rutgers students, to demonstrate against the appearance at Princeton University of Mississippi Governor Ross Barnett, a notorious advocate of segregation. "The Don Harris case has stirred the campus like no other issue in years," reported a *Targum* columnist. The ferment continued until November 1, when Harris was released from jail on bond after a federal court had declared unconstitutional the Georgia statute on which he had been held. He was welcomed back to the campus later that month before returning South to continue his work with SNCC.

The Harris case, together with the general impact of the civil rights struggle in the South, had the effect of activating some concern with race-related matters at Rutgers. It marked the first faint stirring of efforts to increase the black presence on the campus. White consciences had been touched. Soon there were signs, however modest in their immediate consequences, that a new issue was slowly forcing itself onto the crowded agenda of the University.

One such sign was the appointment in September 1963 of a University-level committee to survey the resources that Rutgers might bring to bear on the problems of the disadvantaged. Chaired by Dean Werner W. Boehm of the Graduate School of Social Work, the committee worked conscientiously on its assignment for more than a year. In December, a self-constituted faculty group led by Professor Paul Tillett of the political science department resolved to press for the recruitment of black faculty and students and even envisioned the establishment of a summer remedial program. The Rutgers College Student Council invited Paul Robeson to speak on campus, and the University Senate voted unanimously to call on Congress to enact broad civil rights legislation. At the Commencement in May 1964, an honorary degree was conferred on A. Philip Randolph, the prominent civil rights and labor leader who had been one of the architects of the March on Washington.[2]

Slowly these new evidences of concern began to produce some action. In 1965 the Boehm Committee made its report, setting forth a multifaceted "Equal Opportunity" program. The committee had prepared a preliminary plan, which was

13

reviewed in a series of meetings with two dozen citizens who were involved with minority-group and community-relations projects. The final product, in addition to recommending measures to strengthen community leadership and educate professionals to serve disadvantaged groups, included a "developmental" component. This called for "talent hunts" for disadvantaged students, revision of admission criteria to enhance minority enrollment, enrichment programs at the high school level, special tutorial help, and increases in financial-aid resources. Also proposed were faculty exchanges with predominantly black colleges and seminars for Rutgers instructors to improve their effectiveness in dealing with the special needs and circumstances of the disadvantaged.[3]

The Boehm Report served Rutgers as a general guide for the next three years. In due course, a University Committee (later Council) on Equal Opportunity evolved. Initially its funding was negligible and its effectiveness was dependent on the commitment of individual faculty members and administrators. By 1967, with a vigorous full-time staff person—Dr. Herbert R. Kells—and some allocated funds, the council was operating through several subcommittees and oversaw a growing number of programs for students, staff, faculty, and the community at large. It had yet to confront any determined pressure from black students to accelerate its efforts.[4]

In 1965, Rutgers began to move from expressions of concern and exploratory study to concrete action. In that year the first organized effort to recruit minority students got under way. Faculty and staff volunteers visited five New Jersey high schools, speaking with principals, guidance counselors, and students. By 1967, such contacts were established with fifteen schools. This program raised the number of black undergraduates from around 100 in 1965, to 266 in 1967, and 413 in 1968.[5]

Most of those recruited by this program met ordinary admis-

14

sions requirements, although some were in what was termed a "high risk" category. Especially at Douglass College, there were efforts to provide tutorial help, counseling, and financial aid, as well as reduced course loads, to those students who required such assistance. The Newark College of Arts and Sciences faculty created a Special Entrance Program (SEP) in 1968, and in one year the number of blacks in the college rose from 62 to 140.

Another important new factor was an Upward Bound program, sponsored by the University with funding from the federal Office of Economic Opportunity. By 1968, 150 students from high schools in thirteen cities were enrolled. These students participated in a six-week summer program with follow-up activities during the school year. Beginning in 1967, the second year of the program, several Upward Bound graduates entered Rutgers.[6]

Also under way by 1966 was a move to add more blacks to the faculty, where their numbers were negligible. The provost, the chief academic officer at Rutgers, reserved a number of faculty lines for this purpose, and he made it known that they would be allocated only for minority appointees. A year later fifteen blacks had joined the faculty, and in another year that number was doubled. A similar affirmative action program increased the representation of black staff members.[7]

These early initiatives can best be understood as inspired by the civil rights movement. They had been stimulated by recent federal civil rights legislation and were carried forward chiefly by liberal whites who were in sympathy with the movement. The guiding idea was to eliminate racial barriers by actively recruiting "qualified" black students, faculty, and staff, and by extending appropriate assistance to the black community.

By 1967, some new guiding ideas, dramatically at odds with the reigning ideology of integration, became evident at Rutgers. Black students began to organize for their own

15

betterment and for future action. The widespread civil disorders in scores of northern cities called attention to the limitations of the civil rights movement and lent credence to the new cry for "Black Power." Moreover, the sudden increase in the numbers of black students after 1965 enhanced the effectiveness of their protests against existing conditions. For the first time in the history of Rutgers, there was a critical mass of black students, committed to acting against the racism they perceived within the University.

Representative of the new cohort of black students was Jerome C. Harris, Jr., who entered Rutgers in 1965. He came from a predominantly white Long Island high school where he had excelled in both scholarship and on the track team. Though he expected to encounter hostility on the campus, he had some hope that his obvious qualifications would earn him respect and even acceptance. But like other talented blacks in his class, Harris became frustrated by institutional racism. He came to feel that integration into the dominant white community was "not psychologically or practically satisfying." Forced to deal with the pains of his African-ness and his rejection, he concluded that the civil rights approach was no longer adequate. His thinking turned in a "nationalist" direction. He sought a strategy that could bring about changes in the power relationship in American society. Fortified by these perceptions, he became one of the most influential campus leaders of the black student protest movement.[8]

At Douglass College, Karen Predow arrived at like conclusions. She entered the college in 1966 from Trenton Central High School as one of the early recruits from what became the "Fifteen High Schools Program." A good student who had been prominent in extracurricular activities, she was not in the "high risk" category. Although her fellow students were friendly and considerate, she felt a sense of estrangement. She found herself asking, "How are we different; how are we similar?" She ob-

16

served that many of the white students came from relatively affluent families; their clothes, dating patterns, life styles, and even their academic interests were different. The small number of black women were "always being probed and examined" by the whites; they were looked to as a source of information.

Her discussions of these matters with other blacks at Douglass and Rutgers soon led her toward political action. She read extensively in the contemporary black writings and participated in study groups. She was impressed with the "nationalist" position and by movements in Africa to rescue that continent from white colonialism. She concluded that "There were two movements [civil rights and nationalism], and they were 180 degrees apart." As she later recalled, "You were on one side or the other; you were for Bayard Rustin or Stokeley Carmichael." Predow became one of the black student leaders at Douglass.[9]

Richard W. Roper grew up in Brunswick, Georgia, attended West Virginia State College briefly, then came North to Newark in search of employment. In 1966, he enrolled in the Newark College of Arts and Sciences. He had participated in desegregation efforts in Georgia through the NAACP and in the March on Washington. As Roper saw it, "Black Power was the Northern version of the civil rights movement." He assumed the presidency of the campus NAACP chapter in September 1967, but he and the other members decided that the organization was not the appropriate vehicle to attain their goals. A month later, they returned their charter and formed the Black Organization of Students. "We as idealistic young people felt that the NAACP had served a useful purpose," he explained, "but now it was time to move forward." Like Harris and Predow, Roper was representative of the emerging black student leadership in 1967.[10]

Black student activists recognized the need to mobilize support through appropriate organizations. Late in 1966, several men from Rutgers College attended a meeting at Columbia

17

University sponsored by the Student Afro-American Society (SAS). Representatives were present from several colleges who heard speakers of national prominence expound on the need for black empowerment. The Rutgers contingent returned to the campus inspired, and in December they organized a chapter of SAS, with Frank McClellan as the first president.[11]

SAS was a Rutgers College organization, but women from Douglass participated in its activities during its first year. It sponsored a range of programs. At the outset, a great deal of effort was devoted to providing social events to bring the black community together. Older students were energetic in providing informal counseling to those who had recently been admitted. There were study groups to explore the new intellectual currents. Contacts were established with SAS groups at Princeton, Drew, and Montclair State College and through informal networks with undergraduates at the Newark campus. At the same time, SAS members began thinking about what must be changed at Rutgers and how such changes could best be effected. In March 1968, SAS decided that it should be an all-male organization. The Douglass women formed a Black Students' Committee which focused on local campus grievances while maintaining communication with SAS.[12]

Under its second president, Gene Robinson, SAS formulated its doctrinal position and prepared to assume an activist stance. Robinson, a charismatic leader whose years at Rutgers had been interrupted by military service, was an articulate spokesperson. Writing for a campus publication in March 1968, he explained the meaning of Black Power. The "Civil Rights Revolution," as he saw it, benefited the small black middle class but failed to aid the masses. The recent urban revolts showed the extreme dissatisfaction of the black community with integration and with white cultural values. Robinson applauded the strategy devised by Floyd McKissick, head of CORE, which showed SAS "the way to 'political Black Power' as a new politics

18

of Community Action." At the same time, he rejected the concept of "revolutionary Black Power" espoused by H. Rap Brown.[13]

During these years, a remarkable roster of nationally prominent African American leaders addressed student groups on the New Brunswick campus. They included James Farmer, Roy Innis, and Floyd McKissick of CORE; the Rev. Andrew J. Young of SNCC; Jeremiah Shabazz, Black Muslim minister; the noted authors, Ralph Ellison and Louis Lomax; Dick Gregory, humorist and political activist; Shirley Chisholm, the first black congresswoman, and Muhammad Ali, heavyweight champion. SAS and the student NAACP chapter sponsored symposia on the problems confronting blacks on campus and throughout the nation and on the possible means of addressing them.

The campus newspapers were attentive to racial issues. The Douglass *Caellian,* for example, ran a series of brief pieces for several weeks starting in September 1967, entitled "To Recognize Racism." The author urged the admission of more black undergraduates, the appointment of black faculty, and the introduction of courses relevant to blacks. Later in the year, there were two special issues devoted to "Black Students in a White University," featuring stories on black student organizations and interviews with eight Douglass women. The women told of their discomfort in a white environment and the need they felt to retain their own cultural identity. In March 1968, another speical issue—"Focus: American Minorities"—addressed the plight of Puerto Ricans and American Indians as well as African Americans.[14]

Clearly there was rising sensitivty to racial issues within the University and it was especially evident by 1968. This is not to say that such issues had taken first priority on the agenda of students, faculty, or administrators. Many other matters—the Vietnam War, plans for continued expansion of the University, the new drug culture—all competed for attention. Moreover,

19

while their leaders gave voice to the rhetoric of Black Power, black students in general held a wide diversity of political views. What they shared was the sense that they were strangers in a white-controlled environment, that their numbers were too few, that there was too little in the social and academic spheres with which they could readily identify, and that changes had to be made.

CHAPTER THREE

A New Urgency

I N A CYCLE PECULIAR TO THE ACADEMIC SCENE, April is the month when student activism peaks. Such was the case at Rutgers–New Brunswick in 1968. At Douglass College, there was intense excitement over the issue of abolishing curfew rules, which had long fixed the hours when the women were required to return to their living quarters. On the other side of town, at Rutgers College, there were continuing protests against the Vietnam War. These were further enlivened by a fervent outpouring of support for Sen. Eugene McCarthy in the Democratic presidential primary. Almost invisibly, the University Council on Equal Opportunity was moving forward with its manifold programs to increase the black presence at Rutgers.

Then, on Thursday evening, April 4, the Rev. Dr. Martin Luther King, Jr., was assassinated in Memphis, Tennessee. The nation and the world were shocked, much as they had been by the slaying of President John F. Kennedy five years earlier. Widely respected for his philosophy of nonviolence and his courageous leadership of the civil rights movement, Dr. King was regarded as the outstanding black figure in America. His contributions had brought him the Nobel Peace Prize.

King's death had an unprecedented impact on black students at Rutgers. Malcolm X had been killed, and now Dr. King. No comparable leader remained. The sense of loss was compounded by feelings of pain and anger. "Dr. King's assassination changed everything," one former student recalled. "We realized we would have to carry on the struggle without him, by ourselves. We were shocked into the discovery that we could not just be students anymore." This realization brought African American students together, regardless of previous differences. It inspired them with a sense of urgency; slow progress must give way to rapid, massive change. Their anger suddenly rose; some even spoke of violence.[1]

For a few days the issue of racism seemed to grip the whole campus. On the night of Dr. King's death, black student organizations joined in issuing a statement deploring white apathy. "We black people have reached a breaking point," they declared. "We shall not tolerate this racism any longer. This system must be changed whether with white help or without it."[2] The next afternoon, while white students and officials gathered for memorial services for Dr. King, black students assembled on the Douglass campus. They met briefly with Dean Margery S. Foster, who agreed to consider their request for a course on the history of blacks in America. Then they marched in silent procession across town to the main campus. Here they lowered the American flag, turned it upside down as a sign of their distress, and filed off to Hardenbergh Hall to meet together in their grief.[3]

That evening the Rutgers Student Council convened in an emotional special session with over two hundred and fifty observers in attendance. The council passed a lengthy set of resolutions designed to address the grievances that were being

24

expressed by the black students. A few days later similar resolutions were adopted by the Government Association at Douglass. Over the weekend, a Committee of Concern was formed at the women's college, and a group of graduate students organized an Emergency Committee Against Racism (ECAR). A rally against racism on Saturday night attracted a thousand students, who were aroused by charges that the New Brunswick Housing and Redevelopment Authority was planning to displace hundreds of poor people. On Monday evening, twelve hundred students joined a protest march to show their concern. One observer later described this action as "something very temporary, a single act designed to cleanse the white conscience, nothing more."[4]

All classes were cancelled on Tuesday, the day of Dr. King's funeral. The main campus event that day was a convocation held in the College Avenue Gymnasium. Ten speakers, black and white, including the president of the University, spoke on themes related to racism and on the meaning of recent events. Only a few hundred students attended.[5] On the Douglass campus, house meetings were held to discuss racism. "A lot of the girls just sat there doing their nails or curling their hair," *Caellian* reported. "They didn't want to listen."[6] The Committee of Concern, however, led by Professor Emily Alman of the Sociology Department, used the occasion to organize a campaign to seek the restoration of $100,000 to the state budget. This fund was to be used for tutoring and counseling disadvantaged high school students to prepare them for college. The effort was successful. ECAR created seven subcommittees to work on a range of problems affecting African Americans, both on the campus and in the local community.[7]

During this brief frenzy of white-sponsored demonstrations of concern about racism, black student organizations were reduced to playing a secondary role. Their early statements and actions were little understood, nor were they received without

25

challenges. At the convocation, the president of SAS had set forth
the alternatives available to his predominantly white audience:

> The first choice is, you can all die. You can try to kill off
> the black people as a second choice. The third alternative,
> and the only alternative, is that you can work *for* black peo-
> ple. By working *for* black people I mean taking your goals
> from black people. This is the only way you can have peace
> in this country.[8]

One white student in a letter to *Targum* expressed senti-
ments that were no doubt shared by many others:

1. Bull!
2. Negroes are destroying themselves in their own riots!
3. I'll help anyone who helps himself, and no one who
   demands a gift!

In more sober language, a columnist endorsed many of the
black grievances, but was repelled by the "disconcerting note of
separatist ideology" in their demands. Blacks must understand
that their culture could "serve a valuable purpose *within* the
American society and *not* outside of it."[9]

Within little more than a week, the focus of white student
interest shifted from racism back to the other issues, the most
prominent of which were associated with the Vietnam War.
Black student leaders were not surprised by this turn of events.
It confirmed their belief that if any action was to take place, it
must come as the result of their own efforts. As yet, however,
they had not developed the organization and the strategy to
make their case effectively.

They did succeed in gaining access for the first time to the
Board of Governors of the University. At a regular meeting of
the board on April 11, representatives of SAS appeared, accompanied by an attorney, William Wright, a black alumnus. Also

26

in attendance was Omer Brown, president of the Rutgers College Student Council. Brown reported the resolutions that had been adopted by the council a few days earlier, and the men from SAS and Wright spoke in support of them. The chairman of the board, Archibald S. Alexander, declined to permit a question-and-answer exchange between the students and the board members but stated that the matters that had been presented would be considered at the next meeting. This response was not satisfactory to the delegation, which wanted a commitment that the board would act promptly. At the suggestion of Chancellor Ralph A. Dungan, head of the Department of Higher Education and an *ex officio* member of the board, it was agreed to hold a special evening meeting on April 19 in the University Library to continue the dialogue.[10]

At this extraordinary session, which lasted more than three hours, over seventy black students were present, representing the Black Organization of Students (BOS) at Newark as well as SAS and the Douglass Black Students' Committee. This was the first occasion that the three organizations had been brought together. Prior to the meeting, there had been some informal communication among them. They were quite aware that Bessie N. Hill, for whom they had great regard, was the lone black member of the board, and they did not want their actions to embarrass her. Some of the BOS members met with Hill before they went to New Brunswick, and she told them only to present their demands in an able manner. Within each group, specified individuals were designated as spokespersons.[11]

The students were excited at the prospect of having the opportunity to meet with the most powerful body in the University. Initially, they were somewhat awed by the experience and by the formality of the setting. Demands that were by now becoming familiar were presented and supported by individual student speakers. As the evening wore on, the atmosphere became more contentious. The students perceived that some

board members regarded their presentations as rash, even offen-
sive. The most heated exchange occurred over the demand that
the new Student Center on the College Avenue campus in New
Brunswick be named in honor of Paul Robeson. The students
were told that because of the controversies that had been engendered by Robeson's left-wing political involvements such a des-
ignation would be impolitic; it would injure the University.
They disagreed. No immediate action by the board followed
the dialogue. The blacks had fully aired their grievances, but
they left the meeting with little confidence that the changes
they sought would be made.[12]

In actuality, the pleas of the black students were not entirely
without effect. At its May meeting, the board heard data presented by Malcolm A. Talbott, chair of the Council on Equal
Opportunity, which showed that the University was "only beginning to provide equal employment and enrollment for disadvantaged and minority group members." After discussing the
demands that had been put before them in April, they heard
President Gross describe a budget request to the state to finance special programs and voted $100,000 from their own
reserve fund to be used while awaiting state action. They also
directed Provost Richard Schlatter and other top officials to
meet with the leaders of SAS and report to them what actions
were being taken on the April demands.[13]

Schlatter's report summarized what was being done to enhance the African American presence at Rutgers and what was
being planned. As the result of intensified recruiting efforts in
all divisions, Schlatter predicted that the number of black students would double by September. Similarly, the number of
black faculty would reach thirty, double the current number.
Rutgers had requested $550,000 from the state for minority
programs. Courses in African and African American history
and culture would be increased, and the library would expand
its collections in those areas. The bookstore would add books

and magazines of special interest to blacks. In response to the request that black students who chose to do so be permitted to live together, Schlatter stated that a dormitory section would be made available for that purpose. Approval would also be granted for the establishment of a predominantly black fraternity. College deans would be asked to hold meetings with black student organizations to discuss their grievances. Only on the matter of renaming the Student Center for Paul Robeson did the board reject outright one of the student demands.[14]

There were other promising signs. The faculty of the Law School in Newark voted to reserve 20 places (out of 150) in the entering class for blacks and to waive consideration of law school admission test scores. Twenty-three students were admittd under this program, and a year later the target figure was raised to forty.[15] The Graduate School of Education instituted a Martin Luther King Professorship, which brought eight outstanding black leaders and educators to the University as lecturers during the ensuing academic year. The main library announced plans to enrich its collections of African American literature and history and to mount an exhibit on black culture. Provost Schlatter appointed a talented black assistant, John R. Martin, who assumed his duties June 1. With degrees from Princeton and the Columbia Graduate School of Business, Martin had obtained valuable experience in the state Department of Community Affairs. In 1969, he was to play a key role in formulating a vast new program for disadvantaged students.[16]

The initiatives begun in 1965 were now moving forward. This was the message of a comprehensive report issued by the University Council on Equal Opportunity in the fall of 1968. The council, chaired by Vice-President Talbott and aided by ten subcommittees composed of faculty, students, and administrators, had abruptly accelerated its efforts when Dr. Herbert R. Kells became its secretary and moving spirit late in 1967. As the new academic year began in September 1968, blacks constituted almost 3 percent of the student body, up from 1 percent in 1965. The increase in black faculty was far more dramatic, and there were many new black staff members and administrators, including three members of the admissions staff. Every undergraduate college had some form of "special admissions" or "high risk" program in place. Livingston College, which was to open in 1969, had announced a major commitment to disadvantaged students, along with a focus on urban problems. The several graduate and professional schools were all actively engaged in recruiting black students and faculty. No less significant, the University had committed $854,000 for equal opportunity programs for 1968–1969 and was seeking state funds to enlarge those programs in the following year.[17]

Despite these advances, Kells was anything but complacent. As he saw it, time was running out for American universities, and for Rutgers. "It is painful to realize that we have colleges in New Jersey in urban, even ghetto, areas with no more than a handful of minority group students enrolled," he wrote.[18] Universities were not moving fast enough in preparing themselves to address the educational needs of disadvantaged students. Rutgers was not lagging behind other predominantly white institutions; indeed, it was near the forefront. But time was running out. The black community, and especially black students, were becoming frustrated and angered by the slow pace of progress. For them, time *had* run out. They could be patient no longer. They must take upon themselves the burden of bringing about massive changes.

CHAPTER FOUR

The Breaking Point

*T*HE SUDDEN BURST OF INTEREST in the grievances of the black students at Rutgers in April 1968 was short-lived. Soon an academic year came to an end, and when a new year began, racial issues were not conspiciously high on the University's agenda. Throughout the first semester, black student organizations scrutinized the actions of the administration. Strengthened in numbers by a large influx of freshmen, they deepened their diagnosis of the problems they confronted and developed a communications network among the several campuses. Months passed, and they could see no evidence that the thoroughgoing changes they desired were on the horizon. There were still too few blacks on the faculty or in critical administrative roles. No African American academic programs had been established; cultural events relevant to blacks were meager. Above all, black enrollments had not reached an acceptable level. Frustrated and angered, they concluded that dramatic actions were required to compel the University to address their demands. On each campus, the breaking point was reach in February 1969.

33

THE NEWARK CAMPUS

The Newark campus was the most prominent theater of protest. Located in the heart of a decaying city with a black majority, the overwhelmingly white campus was a vulnerable target. In July 1967, Newark had been ravaged for five days by civil disorders of such alarming proportions that National Guard forces were brought in to restore order. The burning, looting, and shooting left twenty-three dead—twenty-one of them black—and enormous property damage. The episode revealed the frightful feelings of desperation and hostility in the ghetto as well as the callous indifference and incompetence of the corrupt white city administration. It also brought to the fore youthful leaders who saw black empowerment as the essential goal to be pursued within that community.

The main undergraduate unit in Newark was the College of Arts and Sciences. It had twenty-five hundred undergraduates enrolled in 1967, of whom sixty-two were black. A few years earlier there had been no more than twenty. There were no blacks on the faculty. All students commuted to the campus; there were no residence halls. Only a small minority came from Newark.

The faculty of the college was immersed in efforts to solve many pressing problems. It was groping to create a structure of internal governance following the retirement of a dean who had managed affairs for twenty-five years. That dean's successor had been ousted by a faculty revolt after one year. The vice-president in charge of the Newark campus, Malcolm Talbott, was serving as acting dean. There was considerable resentment against the central administration in New Brunswick, which, it was felt, treated Newark like a stepchild. There was also deep concern about maintaining the quality of the student body, for the college was programmed to expand in size at a time when the applicant pool was not increasing.[1]

The college had recently moved from substandard quarters to a new eighteen-acre campus, which it shared with other Rutgers units in Newark. Not all of the facilities envisioned by the faculty had been constructed. When the University obtained funds from a state bond issue late in 1968, the Newark faculty, supported by the student body, made a determined effort to pressure the Board of Governors to alter its priorities and allocate a larger share of the funds to Newark. This issue, rather than the grievances of the black students, was highest on the Newark agenda in 1969.[2]

The black student leaders in Newark had close ties to the Newark community, in which most of them lived. Some had become active politically in the numerous efforts then being made to overthrow the white power structure of the city. In their role as students, they saw themselves as obliged to compel the University to recognize that it must serve the black community in Newark. By the same token, the students felt that they could count on local black organizations to support them in their protests.[3]

One such student leader was Joe Browne. He had grown up in Newark and had attended predominantly white Catholic schools. On the campus he had formed, with Richard Roper, the Black Organization of Students. Colorful in speech and bold in manner, Browne was regarded as one of its more militant members. He dropped out of school for a term to work for VISTA and to participate vigorously in the Newark councilmanic election in November 1968. In the process he learned that "very little can be expected of white folk in Newark . . . other than a move towards greater harassment and repression." As for Rutgers-Newark, he characterized it as "a hallmark of ridiculous, sorrowful, pitiful, arrogant, urban universities." The University was falling far short of meeting its obligations to Newark.[4]

Vicki Donaldson, the most prominent woman in BOS,

remembered her first day on campus. She encountered Richard Roper and thought he must be an African, so few were the blacks at the college. Donaldson had grown up in Florida but moved to Newark in 1967 to live with her mother. She became a member of CORE, joined the campus NAACP chapter, and then moved into BOS, where her intelligence, zeal, and talent for writing quickly elevated her to a leadership position. For her, the 1967 disturbances "created a climate where there was a need to redefine what was significant." It was her conclusion "that programs for our Black people will be for Black progress, by Blacks, through Black self-help."[5]

An important influence on individuals like Browne and Donaldson was Robert Curvin. Curvin had graduated from the college in 1961 after a stint of military service. He then worked for community organizations and became head of CORE in Essex County. While studying for his master's degree at the School of Social Work in New Brunswick, Curvin became affiliated with the Extension Divison of the University in a community leadership training program. In 1968, he was based at the Newark campus in a similar role. As one who knew the college and the Newark community well, he was an obvious choice to be the faculty adviser to BOS. He had very close rapport with the students, who respected and trusted him. Although he did not direct their actions, they relied very heavily on him for advice, information, and guidance.[6]

During the academic year 1967–1968, BOS had made only a slight impact on the campus, in part because many of its members were engrossed with community affairs. They discussed their grievances and met occasionally with Talbott and some faculty members, but they had little visibility prior to the assassination of Dr. King. Then there was a brief manifestation of campus concern, such as had been expressed in New Brunswick. In April, BOS representatives attended the special session of the Board of Governors, where their president, Richard Roper, presented nine "proposals." They called for the recruitment of more black students and faculty; the establishment of new departments of Urban Affairs, Urban Education, and African Affairs; an interdisciplinary institute to study the Newark community; more black literature in the library; and a scholarship fund for Newark students. These demands reflected the commitment of BOS to the Newark community; they were not narrowly focused on items related to the welfare of the students.[7]

The first signs that the faculty was becoming aware of the need to recruit black undergraduates came in the spring of 1968. Under the joint auspices of the Admissions Committee and the Scholastic Standing Committee, faculty members visited high schools and attempted to interest "disadvantaged" students in attending Rutgers-Newark. BOS members volunteered to assist in the program and did so effectively. They were given representation on the Admissions Committee. Black alumni became involved as well. In what was regarded as something of a concession, it was agreed to admit those who ranked in the top 10 percent of the classes in Newark high schools. In furtherance of this initiative, a black man—Lincoln Lawrence—was added to the admissions staff. Altogether ninety disadvantaged students entered the college in September 1968. Only half of them were black.

Although these entrants for the most part met the usual admissions requirements, special courses were arranged in remedial reading and mathematics and in Freshmen English for those who were deemed to be deficient. Only $19,000 was made available to the college for this special program, an amount that the joint committee felt was inadequate. Nevertheless, the experiment was judged a success, and it was continued and expanded a year later as the Special Entrance Program (SEP).[8]

In the fall of 1968, the campus became more fully aware of the presence of BOS through a special issue edited by BOS members of the student newspaper, the *Observer*. Several articles set forth the BOS perspective on the college. Vicki Donaldson expressed her misgivings about the Rutgers Student Volunteer Program (RSVP), an organization of white students that worked in the black community. "I cannot believe that all 'volunteers' really care about Black people," she declared. Harrison Snell, BOS president, denied an allegation that the recently admitted black students meant a lowering of academic standards. "I am appalled that some members of the academic community resent the presence of Black students . . . ," he wrote, "and refuse to admit this resentment but rather hide under the pretext of lower academic standards." Joe Browne went further: "Rutgers should and must be no less than 30 percent Black; a start in this direction would be the admittance of at least 500 Black students for the 1969–70 school year." This would only mark a beginning, according to Browne; innovative actions in many areas would be needed if the institution was to become hospitable to African Americans.[9]

By now, BOS had made its grievances known through many channels. But it had not yet succeeded in gaining the attention of those in a position to redress them. Over the next few months it refined its demands, developed communications with its counterparts in New Brunswick, and debated the strategy it should pursue to gain its objectives. By February it was ready to act.

On February 6, a large delegation from BOS appeared unannounced at a conference of faculty and administrators called by Talbott to discuss admissions. They heard that only twenty-seven of the first one thousand applicants for the coming year were black, a fact of which they were already aware. Thereupon they presented Talbott with a carefully drafted set of twelve demands. They told him that he had two weeks in which to respond.[10]

Malcolm Talbott had the confidence and respect of the BOS leaders. Prior to becoming vice-president at Newark, he had been a professor and associate dean at the law school. He had long been identified with the civil rights movement. He held memberships in the NAACP and the Urban League and served on the New Jersey Committee Against Discrimination in Housing. He chaired the University Equal Opportunity Council. Joe Browne, who looked on him as an ally, said later, "We couldn't have done what we did without Talbott. He was with us." Vicki Donaldson valued Talbott's friendship until he died. She remembered, though, that he was not a good negotiator; whenever he was under pressure his face flushed.

During the grace period, Talbott was engaged almost constantly in conferences with those in the University who must be involved in any decisions regarding the demands. These included President Gross, Provost Schlatter, the Board of Governors, the Council of Deans, the Newark department chairs, the Student Council, and the editor of the *Observer*. On the advice of the department chairs, he did not convene a meeting of the faculty. Instead he met with BOS on February 20 and gave an oral response to the demands. The next morning BOS informed Talbott in writing that his position was "totally unacceptable." A conference with BOS that afternoon produce no agreement. That same day black students held a campus rally as a memorial to Malcolm X. Rumors circulated that the old administration building would be invaded by community activists. University officials in New Brunswick were advised that racial tensions were building on the Newark campus.[11]

These forewarnings reached a climax with the occupation of Conklin Hall on February 24. The seizure was carefully plotted. Key black community organizations were given advance notice so that they could be ready to support the students. BOS obtained detailed plans of the building in preparation for the takeover. Before daylight on February 24, several cars drew up to the building. About twenty-five students carrying food, bedding, tools, and other equipment entered the structure. In less than four minutes they had secured all the entrances with heavy chains. Not until an hour later was their presence discovered. They renamed the building Liberation Hall.[12]

"It was drama! It was exciting! It was frightening! It was very, very awesome!" Thus did one participant remember it. The occupiers were aware of the risk they were taking. They expected to be arrested. But they were far more concerned about a violent confrontation with the Newark police or with the vigilante forces of Anthony Imperiale, a local political figure who was notorious for his hostility toward blacks. Vicki Donaldson confronted the possibility that she might be killed and accepted it.

During the occupation the students slept briefly, talked, read, played cards, issued statements to the press, and made occasional appearances on the roof of the building. They also consulted with BOS representatives who remained outside in order to conduct negotiations with University authorities. For much of the time community groups gathered near Conklin Hall to show their support. There were also hostile elements, such as the Young Americans for Freedom, who denounced the occupation and demanded police action to clear the building. On one occasion a white mob approached the main entrance with a telephone pole, intending to ram open the doors. The rioters were dissuaded from their action by a clergyman.[13]

Never before had there been a building takeover at Rutgers, although such events were becoming commonplace on other campuses. President Gross was adamantly opposed to using force to remove the students; he did not even invoke University policy on dissent, which would have subjected BOS to disciplinary penalties. Gross's leniency was unfavorably contrasted by many critics with the widely applauded stand taken a week earlier by Father Theodore Hesburgh, president of Notre Dame University. Hesburgh had announced that he would give students fifteen minutes to cease their unlawful

40

actions. If they did not yield, they would be expelled from the institution. President Nixon voiced his admiration for Hesburgh's edict.[14]

Gross acknowledged that the students had cause to feel frustrated and angry; be believed that the best course would be to engage in negotiations with them about their grievances. Accordingly, he joined Malcolm Talbott in Newark as an active participant in the protracted discussions, which were held in nearby Ackerson Hall, the Law School building. There they met the BOS representatives and a host of other individuals. These included some members of the faculty; selected students and alumni; Robert Curvin; Gustav Heningburg, a prominent community leader; a reporter for the *New York Post;* and Richard Roper. Roper, who had graduated in June 1968, had joined the staff of Department of Higher Education Chancellor Ralph A. Dungan and served as his observed in Newark.[15]

Agreement was quickly reached on several of the demands. These had to do with hiring additional black personnel, subject to BOS approval, in the admissions and the dean of students offices as well as appointing more black faculty and counselors. There would also be increased funding for remedial programs and scholarships and the early establishment of a Black Studies program. Difficulties arose over the demand that the current director of admissions and his assistant be immediately dismissed, but this awkward matter was partially resolved by transferring the men to other duties. Unhappy with this solution, the clerical staff of the department all resigned.[16]

The most intractable problem had to do with admissions. There were several complications. Gross and Talbott insisted that this matter lay within the prerogative of the faculty, for whom they could not speak. On the other side, BOS altered the specifics of its demand during the course of the negotiations. Moreover, certain BOS proposals were so explicit with regard to race or geography as to be open to legal challenges. Such was

41

the case, for example, with the proposal that no black applicant with a diplomna from a Newark high school could be rejected prior to September 1. It would be futile—and serve little purpose—to trace the tangled course of negotiations on this central issue. Suffice it to say that by the early morning of February 27, BOS believed that it had achieved a "signed agreement" with Gross that met its requirements. At 5:45 a.m. seventy-two hours after the occupation had begun, the students marched out of Conklin Hall, seemingly in triumph.[17]

The precise content of the alleged agreement on the admissions question cannot be determined. BOS members believed they had won a virtual open-admissions policy for black students from Newark high schools. They had been told repeatedly that only the faculty could act in this area. They had been informed that the admissions committee had recently adopted the practice of considering seriously for admittance Newark black students who had graduated in the top half of their class or who had verbal SAT scores of at least 400. They had been asked to regard this statement as private and informal, not as a public declaration of policy. The faculty was averse to giving formal sanction to a *policy* that was racially and geographically discriminatory, even though it would informally condone the *practice*. Subsequent charges, countercharges, and recriminations did nothing to clarify the issue.[18]

With the evacuation of Conklin Hall, the spotlight now shifted to the faculty. They received conflicting information about the terms of the "agreement," and in any case did not feel that they were necessarily bound by it. A conference between BOS representatives and members of the faculty and administration on March 1 failed to resolve the misunderstandings. At one point BOS insisted on the admission of all black graduates of Newark high schools. The faculty was not averse to increasing black enrollment, but a majority felt strongly that any ad-

42

mission standard must be colorblind. Too, there were misgivings about giving preference to one geographic area, such as Newark. The fear that the college would be swamped by students with poor qualifications, which could mean the rejection of those with superior records, was also present. Many of the faculty felt keenly that they should not appear to be acting under duress and that they should guard closely their authority with respect to admissions policy.[19]

All of these considerations were evident when the faculty convened on March 6 to consider a carefully crafted report from the Admissions Committee. According to this document, it would be the policy of the college to "consider seriously all disadvantaged applicants . . . who are in the top 50 percent of their graduating class or who have a verbal [SAT] score of 400 or more" for the Special Entrance Program (SEP). The number of applicants admitted to SEP would be governed by the availability of resources. After lengthy debate, this policy was adopted by a vote of 95–40. Acting Dean Talbott asked that his vote be recorded in the negative and stated that he now understood how Woodrow Wilson felt when the Senate rejected the League of Nations. The faculty then adopted a resolution to encourage minority alumni to participate in the recruitment process. As might have been predicted, the new policy was colorblind, embodied no geographical restrictions, and implied that there would be limits on the number of applicants accepted into the SEP. Predictably, too, BOS utterly rejected the formula.[20]

The faculty also sought to meet another demand that BOS had raised during the negotiations concerning scholastic standing regulations. It agreed that no student would be dismissed for academic reasons until he or she had completed thirty-two credits and that the grades for the first sixteen credits would not be calculated in a cumulative average. In other actions the faculty granted approval for the establishment of programs in Afro-American Studies and Urban Studies.[21]

Still, the critical admissions issue remained a source of contention. The faculty policy fell far short of BOS's minimal demand that the college *accept* (not merely *consider*) black Newark high school graduates who met the stated criteria. The fact that only limited numbers would be accepted and that "disadvantaged" applicants, regardless of race, would make up the quota, was also objectionable. At a press conference on Saturday, March 8, Joe Browne announced that because the University had "reneged" on its alleged agreement respecting admissions, all terms of that agreement were now "null and void." Browne had just succeeded the scholarly and moderate Harrison Snell as head of BOS, and he made it plain that he was prepared to take "drastic measures" to attain the group's objectives.[22]

The nature of those measures became evident on the following Thursday, March 13. BOS, in conjunction with a hastily organized Concerned Students' Coalition that included Students for a Democratic Society (SDS), staged a rally in the center of the campus. As about three hundred protesters gathered, a large bonfire was ignited in front of the Dana Library. Within minutes, firetrucks were on the scene, and a struggle ensued between the demonstrators and the firefighters. With police assistance, the firefighters succeeded in extinguishing the blaze.

While they were doing so, several BOS members and their supporters invaded Talbott's office and demanded that the college be shut down. Talbott refused. The rally was then resumed in Conklin Hall, where Browne declared that BOS would close the school starting the next morning. Other speakers, including community activists, applauded this new tactic and denounced the administration. Plans were made to bring in busloads of Newark high school students to augment the demonstration.

That evening faculty and student leaders met and decided that the disorders and threats of violence were serious enough to warrant the cancellation of classes and recommended such action to President Gross. At 1:00 a.m. Friday morning, Gross reluctantly agreed.[23]

This new turn of events met with little support among the predominantly white student body. At the time of the Conklin Hall takeover, both the Student Council and the *Observer* had expressed qualified support for BOS and its demands. A crude poll, however, indicated that a majority of the students were opposed to the seizure of the building. SDS and other small leftist groups sided with BOS, while the Young Americans for Freedom provided the most vocal opponents. The activities and statements on March 13, and especially the threat to close down the campus, shocked and angered most of the student body. An *Observer* columnist drew parallels between BOS and the Hitler Youth. Student Council declared that what was now at stake was "not the morality or philosophy of BOS's demands but the existence of our University." Fearing violence and bodily harm, they condemned BOS and urged all students to remain calm and not force a confrontation.[24]

For more than a month the Newark campus had been in turmoil. What was perceived to be the militancy of BOS frightened many students and faculty, although there were no violent incidents. They dreaded the possible invasion of the campus by aroused local supporters of BOS, which included the Black Panthers. Despite the fact that no damage had been done to Conklin Hall and classes held in that building had been rescheduled promptly in other facilities, there was wide resentment about the inconvenience caused by the occupation.

Black students were no less fearful of police intervention and of threats by white students to take the law into their own hands. They were conscious, too, that they were acting not only for themselves but for the Newark black community, and this sensibility made them unwilling to moderate what they regarded as their justifiable demands. To do so would be a betrayal of their Newark constituency. Heightening the sense of crisis was the extensive media coverage of the prolonged confrontation, which featured many statements and letters condemning the University for failing to maintain order.

Thus by mid-March profound differences, exacerbated by rising tensions, polarized the Newark campus. The faculty had taken a stand on the admissions issue from which it was unlikely to budge. Bos had adopted a position that it would hold to even if this required the closing of the school. It was in this highly charged atmosphere that the Board of Governors was to meet on March 14 and bring forth a surprising solution to the Newark problem.

NEW BRUNSWICK

Protest actions by African American students at Rutgers College and Douglass College early in 1969 took quite a different form from those in Newark. So, too, did the responses to those protests. "At Newark," as Jerry Harris analyzed it, "the student movement was an outgrowth of what was happening in the community." At Rutgers and Douglass, although the students were not without ties to their own communities, they were not much involved with affairs in New Brunswick. Their demands were campus-centered. In both colleges primary responsibility for dealing with the black students' agenda was assumed by the faculties, rather than by administrators. There were no building seizures, protracted negotiations, or accusations of violated agreements.

Rutgers College

At Rutgers College as the new academic year began in September 1968, there were 95 black students out of a total enrollment of 6,416. Thirty-eight were freshmen. There were 3 blacks on a faculty that numbered 558. Few fully "qualified" blacks were applying for admission, in part because so many other Northern colleges and universities were now conducting recruitment campaigns. Even the pool of "high risk" applicants was not growing, despite the efforts put forth in the "Fifteen High Schools Program." Aside from modest tutorial funds, there was little semblance of an academic support program, nor were there provisions for reduced courseloads. The creation of a major in Black Studies was under consideration, despite strong reservations expressed by the dean. Cultural activities appealing to blacks were negligible. The sole tangible outcome of the demands that had been made the previous April was the authorization of a "black section" in Clothier dormitory, occupied by twenty-three black and four white students. Even though the University had allocated $850,000 for its "Equal Opportunity" thrust——most of it for financial aid and faculty and staff hiring—the results seemed meager. As a skilled reporter on the national scene put it succinctly: "The effort at Rutgers thus far has increased the prospect of change more than it has produced change itself."[25]

The Student Afro-American Society was quite aware of the slow pace of change, but it maintained a low profile throughout the fall semester of 1968. It was trying to strengthen its internal unity; there were still black students who remained aloof because they lacked sympathy with the political orientation of the SAS leadership. It was also a period when prolonged discussions were under way regarding strategy and tactics. What risks were inherent in various possible actions? How should SAS relate to SDS or other white allies? Should each

47

college group act independently, or should there be coordinated movement? What specific demands and proposals should be presented and what factual data was required to back them up? Above all, how could the dominant white academic community be brought to recognize, if not fully understand, the needs and aspirations of the African American minority?[26]

By the fall of 1968, new leaders were coming to the fore in SAS, most of whose members were now underclassmen. The seniors in the group decided that any major changes that might be initiated would have to be implemented over a period of several years. Therefore it would be desirable to install younger men in key positions so that they could monitor future developments.[27]

Under these circumstances Leon Green became head of SAS. A native of Alabama, he had moved with his family to Newark when he was twelve years old. He held a succession of after-school jobs to supplement welfare checks. At the age of fourteen Green became a licensed preacher, a vocation he had followed since the age of eight. Serious-minded and intelligent, he was a good student and had always believed that he would go to college, even though his guidance counselor urged him to become a school janitor. He entered the Upward Bound program after his junior year at West Side High School, and this opportunity gave him his first introduction to Rutgers. It also taught him that students from his background must be prepared to face the cultural, as well as the educational challenge of entering a predominantly white institution.

As a freshman in 1967, Green was struck by the alien environment in which he and his classmates found themselves. He encountered racial slurs and epithets. He found little difference between life in the ghetto and on the campus. "Our very presence produced antagonism." Blacks, it seemed, were expected to "meld into the regular campus milieu; no consideration was given to their social or cultural needs." "If you feel that you can

48

be nothing unless you belong to a group that doesn't want you," he concluded, "then psychologically you can easily be crippled. If you think that you can be something independent of the other group, then you can feel better." An admirer of both Dr. King and Malcolm X, he was especially attracted by the latter's insistence that African Americans must build their own identity within their own community.

Green joined SAS as a freshman, but not until the death of Dr. King did he regard its mission as urgent. When he assumed the leadership of the organization in the late fall of 1968, he established a strong committee structure, began methodically to collect information on every relevant aspect of college and University operations, and weighed alternative courses of action. Rejecting the offer of SDS to join with SAS in violent confrontations, he groped toward a tactic that would be both morally correct and effective.[28]

While Leon Green concentrated on Rutgers College problems, Jerry Harris—now a senior—continued to play an extremely influential role in a larger setting. He had become one of the students actively involved in planning for Livingston College, which was to have a special commitment to minority students. Because of contacts that he had made in Newark and Camden, Harris was a critical link in the relationship among the several campuses. His apartment, shared with his classmate Charles "Chuck" Bowers, became the communications center for the movement. It was here that important planning sessions took place, manifestoes were mimeographed, and decisions were made. Ironically, the apartment was in the basement of the residence occupied by the University dean of student affairs, Earle Clifford, with whom Harris had a good relationship as a student and a tenant.[29]

By February, black student organizations at Newark, New Brunswick, and Camden had agreed that it was now time to act. Pressure would be brought to bear on each college and, through the colleges collectively, on the University. It was left up to each organization to determine how it would secure attention to its demands. However, to achieve the maximum impact, the various demonstrations were to take place within a limited time span.

The first move in New Brunswick was a modest one, a request by Jerry Harris in the name of an ephemeral Black Unity League for a house that could serve as a center for coordinating the activities of all black groups on the New Brunswick campus. "There is no dogma of 'separation' governing the idea of this center," Harris assured Dean Clifford, to whom the request was directed. There was no immediate response from the administration.[30]

Far more consequential was a letter addressed by SAS to the dean of Rutgers College, Arnold B. Grobman, on February 12. The letter pointed out that a list of grievances and proposals had been put forth the previous April. The result had been several meetings, along with assurances that actions would follow. Now SAS called on the dean and faculty to report on what had actually been accomplished. Specific information was requested regarding students admitted, financial aid, number of black faculty and staff hired, number of courses in Afro-American Studies added, the status of plans for a summer program in 1969, and the names of college committees responsible for these areas of concern. The dean was given two weeks to provide such a comprehensive accounting. A week later the Rutgers College Student Council endorsed a report issued jointly by SAS and the Emergency Committee Against Racism (ECAR) that criticized the administration for its failure to establish an Afro-American Studies department. There were also rumblings about harsh disciplinary action taken against a black undergraduate, "Buzzy" Green. The campus became pervaded by the sense that racial tensions were reaching a critical point.

On the morning of February 24 came the ominous news that BOS had occupied Conklin Hall.[31]

The next evening, a Tuesday, protest erupted in New Brunswick. About fifty black students filed into the main dining hall, filled their trays with food, threw them on the floor, and silently departed. By prearrangement, there was a similar demonstration at Douglass College. White students were startled; some were outraged and shouted nasty comments at the demonstrators. On the following evening, the black students all ate together and then stood in a group on the balcony overlooking the dining area. A confrontation seemed imminent, but the blacks left before any incident developed. The next day there was a rash of acts of vandalism, bomb threats, and minor fires. Protective screening was hastily installed to safeguard the main telephone switchboard and the computer system. The campus was rife with alarming rumors.[32]

Earlier in the year the faculty had created a Community Action Committee (CAC) made up of students and faculty. Its mission was to be alert to situations that might lead to explosive behavior and to recommend ways of dealing with them. CAC immediately began a dialogue with students in the "black section," seeking to assess the magnitude of the crisis. The blacks vented their outrage. "Last weekend there were whites screaming 'nigger' up to the section. . . . We're tired of being 'niggers,' of taking the bullshit. . . . Everybody has a breaking point; you can push only so far. . . . We're sick of talking. . . . We want something done on our grievances." On Wednesday evening, after a lengthy and tense meeting with the protesters, Dean Grobman was persuaded to cancel classes on Friday, Monday, and Tuesday, a move that had the endorsement of CAC.[33]

CAC assumed responsibility for arranging an array of workshops and "sensitivity sessions" to air not only the blacks' grievances but also other issues of concern to students, such as curricular reforms and enhanced student power. At a convocation in the gymnasium on Friday afternoon an overflow audience of 2,800 heard Randy Green, a black freshman, give a powerful speech. Its message, briefly stated, was: "This place has got to change, or we're going to leave." In the workshops that followed, black issues received less attention than did the efforts of a radical caucus of white students to use the occasion to advance its own agenda. Yet another faction was intent on pressing for the adoption of the far-reaching innovations proposed by Professor Warren Susman for the reconstruction of the college's curriculum.[34]

Of greater consequence was an informal meeting of nearly a hundred members of the faculty on Sunday evening. Those present agreed that before administrators made any commitments to the black demands—which had not yet been presented by SAS—the faculty should have an opportunity to consider them. A petition was sent to the dean requesting him to convene a special faculty meeting as soon as possible. Behind this unusual move lay the conviction that only the faculty had the authority to take the kinds of actions that would be needed to address the anticipated demands. There was an awareness, as well, of the difficulties that were being encountered in Newark, where University officials had taken the lead in negotiations.[35]

The next steps took place swiftly. On Monday evening, in the presence of SAS members, their attorney, William Wright, and a large throng of students and faculty, Dean Grobman presented the "progress report" that had been requested some two weeks earlier. He did not have much progress to report, but he noted that several matters were under study by relevant committees. He did announce that Wright could formally present the SAS demands at a faculty meeting at 10:00 a.m. the following day.[36]

The meeting, held in the gymnasium, was a dramatic event. Seated on the main floor were nearly three hundred members of the faculty. To one side were most of the African American students in the college, many of then arrayed in dashikis. The balconies were filled with white student observers. Wright, in a calm but forceful manner, presented the demands, which were further explained by five student speakers. The faculty then resolved that it would not place any other items on its agenda until matters related to these demands had been addressed. It authorized the appointment of a Select Committee and charged it with preparing recommendations to be brought before the faculty in a session that same evening.[37]

The Select Committee began its work ten minutes later. Made up of the members of the Community Action Committee; three appointed faculty members; and the dean, dean of men, and director of admissions as *ex officio* members, the committee was chaired by Professor Richard P. McCormick of the Department of History. Meeting simultaneously in the same building were standing committees of the college that worked jointly with the Select Committee and members of the dean's staff throughout the afternoon. When the faculty convened at 7:20 p.m., the Select Committee was prepared to present a report that embodied statements and resolutions on all of the demands that were within its province.[38]

The knottiest problem that had faced the Select Committee was that of increasing black enrollments. Under existing regulations, no applications for admission could be accepted after February 1. The best estimate was that no more than forty blacks would be entering as freshmen in September. In order to reopen admissions but restrict the process to "disadvantaged" students, the solution adopted was to announce a new "Transitional Year Program" (TYP). This would be a residential program for "high risk" students who would take a combination of remedial (noncredit) and regular courses until they were prepared for full matriculation. Every effort would be made to enroll one hundred students in this program, including the

53

prompt hiring of two black recruiters and the payment of stipends to black student recruiters. Tied in with the TYP would be a six-week summer program, headed by a black director.

Other resolutions called for the appointment of fifteen black faculty during the ensuing year, the hiring of a black assistant dean and financial aid officer, and the naming of blacks to relevant college committees. The faculty was also asked to endorse an Afro-American Studies program, a Black Experience course, additional funding for cultural activities, and the acquisition of works by contemporary black authors by the University Library. Because black students complained of being harassed by campus security officers, a faculty-student grievance committee would be established to hear any charges of unfair treatment. Other recommendations, not of exclusive interest to blacks, called for more flexible course-loads, the assurance that no student would be dismissed for academic deficiencies before completing two semesters, pass-fail grading for a student's first semester, and the omission of freshman grades from the cumulative average. All of the resolutions and recommendations of the Select Committee were adopted without any recorded dissent.

William Wright said he was "overwhelmed with the support and concern the Faculty . . . had shown to the demands that had been made." As the three-hour meeting drew to a close, the entire assemblage gave a standing ovation to Wright and to the black students. The ovation signified that the impetus for essential changes had come from a group of dedicated, informed, and able undergraduates who had set aside their personal academic goals to achieve a larger vision.[39]

Over the next two weeks the Select Committee met with a committee of black students led by Leon Green and with college and University administrators to ensure that the actions taken by the faculty would be implemented. The students were by now well informed about the operations of the college and in a position to make vital proposals in such areas as financial aid, admissions, staffing, and recruitment. Many of them later devoted the spring recess to recruiting applicants for the Transitional Year Program. Others participated in interviewing prospective appointees to faculty and staff positions. Whatever good will had been manifested by the faculty was fully matched by that of the students.

Late in May a crisis arose when it appeared that there would not be adequate funds to finance the TYP. The black students were understandably irate and charged a betrayal of the commitments that had been made in March. This feeling was shared by the faculty, which met in an emergency session on May 28 and adopted strong resolutions insisting on University support for the TYP. To evidence its deep concern, it adopted a proposal that faculty members be asked to contribute one percent of their salaries. Over $25,000 was raised in this manner. In June, the Board of Trustees and the Board of Governors drew on reserve funds to make it possible for the special programs to go forward.[40]

For a few hectic weeks, the college had been compelled to address the long-standing grievances of a small group of students. Very quickly after the three-day interlude of workshops and sensitivity sessions, most undergraduates turned their attention to the less troubling but more exciting diversion of basketball. The team had won sixteen straight games and was headed for the National Invitational Tournament. The faculty resumed its complex political manuvering over the highly controversial proposals of Professor Susman for restructuring the college. SDS criticized the feebleness of the faculty's attack on racism and resumed its manifold challenges to established authority. The college scene remained lively, but race-related issues once again receded into the background.

Douglass College

By 1968, Douglass College had made more progress in recruiting and meeting the needs of African American students than any of the other undergraduate units at Rutgers. For two decades after it was founded in 1918, there were no black graduates; down to 1965 there were fewer than fifty. But in 1968 115 black students were among the 2,860 women enrolled in the college. Nearly two-thirds of them had been "special admits" because they were regarded as economically or educationally disadvantaged, but their academic profiles were not markedly different from those who had been regularly accepted. The faculty made it possible for them to take five years to gain their degrees and offered them tutorial and counseling services as well as financial aid. The Douglass Equal Opportunity Committee under the leadership of Professor Emily Alman was more vigorous than the similar committees in the other colleges and could call on a large number of faculty members for volunteer services as recruiters and advisers.[41]

Despite these advances, the black women at Douglass were not without grievances. These centered less on the area of admissions than on the oppressively white milieu in which they found themselves. They were, in general, less militant and less separatist than the men at Rutgers College, but they shared the sense of being in an alien environment dominated by white cultural attitudes. With the formation of the Douglass Black Students' Committee (DBSC), they had an organization that could bring them together, establish their identity, and voice their distress. Like SAS, the DBSC had made its grievances known at the time of Dr. King's assassination and had participated in the April 19 meeting with the Board of Governors. As the first semester of the new academic year passed with no discernable response, feelings of frustration rose.

The deficiencies that the DBSC observed at Douglass were glaring. There was but one black on a faulty of nearly two hundred. There was one black counselor, whose duties involved advising all commuting students. Black administrators, even black secretaries, were lacking. There were no courses in black history and few curricular offerings that dealt with the black experience in America aside from two in literature. There was a dearth of cultural programs. All of these grievances had been aired in April 1968, and they had been reemphasized by DBSC through Karen Predow and other spokeswomen in October. How much longer must they wait for action?

By the second semester their patience was at an end. Discussions with college administrators had been unproductive. They were told of budgetary problems, of the difficulty of finding fully qualified black professors, of the possibility that a strong program in Afro-American Studies would be developed at Livingston College. Meanwhile, DBSC leaders were conferring with the black student organizations at the other colleges and planning with them a coordinated attempt to bring about change within the University. As BOS and SAS made their initial moves early in February, DBSC prepared to join in.[42]

On Friday, February 21, *Caellian* published a letter from DBSC that made the campus aware that a crisis was at hand. The letter charged that the dean of the college, Margery S. Foster, had failed to hire a particular black woman as a counselor for implausible reasons. It then went on to charge that Foster "does not find it necessary to deal with the Douglass blacks as a legitimate segment of the college community." She did not treat them with "common courtesy" and she put forth "deliberate untruths." This was strong language, but there was more to follow. The demands that had been made almost a year earlier had been ignored. "We shall not tolerate the disregard of our demands and the treatment which we have received from members of the Douglass community," the statement continued.

57

"We are forced to take action to insure the fulfillment of the needs of the black students at Douglass."[43]

Hurriedly the Equal Opportunity Committee prepared a "fact sheet" for distribution to faculty and students, detailing what had been done for African Americans in such areas as admissions, faculty recruitment, tutoring, and curriculum. This document formed the basis for a report that Dean Foster made at a meeting with DBSC on Tuesday afternoon. The students were not impressed. That evening, like their counterparts at Rutgers College, sixty of them overturned their trays in the college's dining halls. On the next day, there were numerous related incidents. Blacks abruptly walked out of classes, yelled insults at instructors, locked bathroom doors and clogged drains. They refused to speak with white students and declined to meet with the dean for further discussions. On Friday they distributed leaflets charging that the University had been unwilling to deal with their problems. "Blacks can no longer tolerate this," they declared.[44]

White students were stunned; many of them were angry. Why wouldn't the blacks communicate? (They felt they had but that they had not been heard.) Why were the blacks behaving so outrageously? (Polite discussion had availed them nothing.) When Dean Foster decided to follow the example of Rutgers College and cancel classes for three days, white resentment increased. Faculty members were disturbed by what they saw as a white backlash. "Formerly sympathetic whites are not so sympathetic anymore," one observed.[45]

In the midst of the turmoil, Foster came to an agreement with DBSC not only to cancel classes but also to set up six committees to consider their concerns. While these committees were at work, students would attend workshops on Monday and Tuesday to discuss racial issues. The six committees, all of which included black students, dealt with admissions, scholarships, counseling, personnel, curriculum, and lectures.[46]

At a special meeting on Thursday, March 6, the faculty received and discussed the reports of the six committees. Five days later at a second meeting all of the twenty-five recommendations made by the committees were approved with only minor modifications. Nine of the proposals were fully within the competence of the faculty, nine others depended for their implementation on other agencies of the University, and the remainder dealt with initiatives that were already in process. The six committees continued at work on the monitoring of the faculty actions until this important function was taken over by an Equal Opportunities Board early in the next academic year.[47]

One of the key recommendations was that ninety-six spaces should be reserved in the incoming class for black applicants, even if this meant curtailing out-of-state admissions. Every effort would be made to appoint fifteen black faculty members over the next two years, as well as a black assistant dean, a black counselor-in-residence, and black professionals in admissions and financial aid. An Afro-American Studies program would be approved, and an African American residence similar to the foreign-language houses would be established. The summer orientation program would be lengthened from two to six weeks. Several suggestions from DBSC regarding cultural programming were also adopted. By the following October the Equal Opportunities Board was able to report that twenty-three of the faculty actions had been implemented or were in progress.[48]

The reaction of the Douglass black students was mixed. They acknowledged that the faculty's response to their demands was gratifying, but they regretted that it had been necessary for them to devote so much of their time and energy to effecting the changes. "I'd like to see this as the last time we'll have to do something like this to make progress," one remarked. Another pointed out that "many of these changes could have been instituted without all this extra to-do." White students were relieved that the crisis had passed, although some continued to feel aggrieved by the methods used by DBSC to gain the attention of the college community.[49]

For many reasons, the black student protest and its consequences were less traumatic at Douglass than at the other undergraduate colleges. The demands were more manageable, the procedures that were followed in addressing them were more judicious, and—because of steps that had been taken previously—the pressures on the faculty were less intense. Douglass was a more closely knit community than either the Newark College of Arts and Sciences or Rutgers College; it had a tradition of good relations between faculty and students. This tradition served it well in its time of crisis.

CAMDEN

Camden, like Newark, was a deteriorated city whose public school population was predominantly African American and Puerto Rican. It presented a landscape of dismal slums and blighted industrial areas surrounding a shrinking mercantile district. Located on a small campus near the heart of the city in attractive new buildings was a School of Law and an undergraduate unit, the College of South Jersey (CSJ). These had been small proprietary institutions until 1950, when they were taken over by Rutgers University. All of the students were commuters, and most of those in CSJ came from Camden and nearby South Jersey counties.

The college in September 1968 enrolled nearly twelve hundred undergraduates, of whom only seventeen were black. Within a faculty of about one hundred, there were only three black academic professionals. Three of the 150 law school students were black. Not until 1968 was there an effort to recruit black students through the "Fifteen High Schools" program, and the results had not been impressive. The college was even less involved with the Camden community than its Newark counterpart, although a Community Advisory Board was created in December 1968, and students were engaged in a tutoring program for schoolchildren.[50]

The impetus for the black student protests at the College of South Jersey came from the black community in the city. Community activists had formed the Black People's Unity Movement (BPUM) as a power base from which to combat the white political structure. As an offshoot of this organization, black undergraduates in September 1967 created the Black Student Unity Movement (BSUM). The BSUM remained relatively dormant until late in 1968 when, with strong encouragement from the BPUM and some contact with black student groups in the other divisions of the University, it became active.

Working closely with advisers from the BPUM, the small membership of BSUM compiled a lengthy agenda of twenty-four demands. These were mimeographed and distributed around the campus on February 10.[51] Only one of the demands dealt directly with admissions; it said simply that the college should recruit 250 black students. Several of the items proposed what would have amounted to a black subcollege within CSJ, with a black dean of students, director of admissions, and director of financial aid; a board of academic inquiry; an urban education department; a black studies department; credit for black life experience; a black section in the library; and a black dormitory.

The BSUM insisted that the college should serve the Camden black community. This meant establishing an educational cultural center, creating a community foundation with initial funding of $50,000, and providing the community with access to University facilities. The BSUM also called for the removal of

61

racist professors, a course in racism, graduate programs in fields other than law and education, reduced teaching loads and increased pay for professors, the setting up of a night preparatory division for high school dropouts, and the naming of a library addition for Paul Robeson.

Two days later the black leaders met with a group of administrators and faculty to explain their demands. They indicated that they were prepared to accept three monthly progress reports, the first of which was to be presented February 17. This report, prepared by the administration, was made on schedule and was immediately declared unacceptable. The BSUM interrupted an outdoor meeting held by the Student Council, burned a copy of the response, and insisted that President Gross come to Camden and meet with them. Over the next few days Earle Clifford, University vice-president for student affairs, met twice with the black students and with faculty members, seeking information that he could relay to Gross.[52]

Gross went to Camden on February 26, at the height of the Newark negotiations. He met first with six members of the BSUM and left them with the impression that he endorsed their demands. But in his remarks immediately afterward before the whole college, he appreared to qualify his position. To demonstrate their anger, the black students left the meeting en masse. That evening, about ten of them, joined by several members of the Camden community, entered the College Center, barricaded themselves inside, and let it be known that they would not depart until their demands were met.[53]

Throughout the night members of the college's Dissent Policy Board carried on negotiations with the occupiers of the College Center. The protesters agreed to leave the building when they received an acceptable written response from President Gross, who was then engaged in discussions with BOS in Newark. He hurriedly dispatched a letter to the Camden demonstrators, and they peaceably vacated the building shortly after noon on February 27.[54]

The president's statement met the substance of most of the twenty-four demands, although it was couched in different terms and made implementation of several items contingent on the availability of funds from public and private sources. In essence, he agreed that every effort would be made to recruit more black students, appoint more black faculty and staff, incorporate courses relevant to African Americans in the curriculum, and make the college more accessible to the Camden community. He concluded by saying that it would be up to the faculty and staff of the college to accept responsibilty for executing these plans as rapidly as possible.

Because of the turmoil on campus, classes were cancelled for three days as they were elsewhere in the University. During this interim, there were workshops, assemblies, and meetings of faculty committees to consider the black demands. Reports and recommendations from these sessions were made available to the faculty before it convened on March 6 to express its own response to the BSUM.[55]

The week-long discussion made it evident to all concerned that the demands were not to be taken literally, that some of them so violated acceptable legal and academic norms as to be infeasible. What was required was evidence of good will and understanding in making the college more hospitable to an augmented black presence. It was in this context that the faculty acted. It voted to endorse "the spirit and basic principles of the demands" while expressing serious reservations about a few of them. It gave its approval to trying to establish a major in urban studies and black studies, but left unclear the form that such programs would take. The faculty pledged to recruit more black students and to keep admissions open until September 1, but no quotas were set and no changes were made in

63

requirements. Most other matters were left to administrative action or were so reinterpreted as to appear to be already in the process of accomplishment.[56]

Unquestionably the college had been shaken by the black students' protests, but the tangible results fell far short of those registered in Newark and New Brunswick. No special programs, such as TYP or SEP, were created; there was no relaxation of scholastic regulations. In part this was due to the nature of the twenty-four demands. Some of them were vague, as in the area of admissions; some were too extreme, such as were those asking for a black subcollege; others, like that requesting a black dormitory, were contrary to law and to University policy. The relative inexperience of the leaders of the BSUM was also a factor in producing such limited results at Camden. Massive reform was to come only in the wake of significant new policy decisions by the Board of Governors.

James Dickson Carr, the first African American graduate of Rutgers College in 1892.

Donald S. Harris, RC '63, whose jailing in Americus, Georgia, in August 1963, ignited interest in the civil rights movement at Rutgers.

Inverting the flag on the Douglass College campus as a sign of distress following the assassination of the Rev. Dr. Martin Luther King, Jr., April 5, 1968.

Richard W. Roper, Newark-Rutgers '68, first president of the Black Organization of Students (BOS).

Vicki Donaldson, Newark-Rutgers '71, prominent spokesperson for the Black Organization of Students.

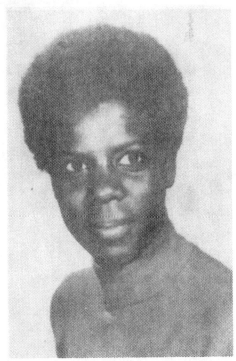

Karen Predow-James, DC '70, chair of the Douglass Black Students Committee.

Leon Green, RC '71, president of the Student Afro-American Society.

BOS protesters, Newark Campus, February 1969.

BOS occupies Conklin Hall and renames it Liberation Hall, February 24, 1969.

Young Americans for Freedom protest against the occupation of Conklin Hall.

Freshman Randy Green addresses a rapt audience in the College Avenue Gymnasium, February 28, 1969.

Attorney William Wright, RC '50, Charles Bowers, RC '69, and Jerome C. Harris, Jr., RC '69, confer during presentation of demands to Rutgers College faculty, March 4, 1969.

Ten years later: Black students protest on the New Brunswick campus, 1979.

CHAPTER FIVE

"A New and Pioneering Program"

I N MID-MARCH 1969, the University's Board of Governors made a surprising decision to introduce "a new and pioneering program" for disadvantaged students. By that time the faculties of the four major undergraduate colleges had all taken action in response to the demands of black student organizations. At Rutgers College and Douglass College the proceedings had drawn little public notice, and the reforms that were set in motion were essentially acceptable to those who had mounted the protests. At Camden, where a building had been occupied only briefly, the campus soon resumed normal operations.

Conditions were different at Newark. The three-day occupation of Conklin Hall and the prolonged negotiations with the Black Organization of Students had been reported extensively in the media and had provoked hostile reactions. The rejection by BOS of the terms offered them by the faculty of the College of Arts and Sciences and their resumption of disruptive activities resulted in chaos. On March 14, all classes were cancelled. While blacks clamored for the full acceptance of their demands, campus opinion turned against them, and around the state citizens and public officials called for strong measures to restore order.

It was against this background that the Board of Governors met in New Brunswick on the morning of March 14. On its agenda were a familiar array of matters related to finances, personnel, and the construction program. But the recent incidents at Newark required immediate attention. The evening before the board meeting, Chancellor Dungan had gone to Newark and spent several hours in discussions with the protesting students and with members of the faculty and administration. He was impressed with the gravity of the situation, as was President Gross. Somehow a way had to be found to end the crippling impasse.

The board went immediately into executive session to consider the latest crisis. Chancellor Dungan startled his colleagues by recommending that Rutgers "admit into its regular programs all disadvantaged students who apply, wherever they came from, and then press very hard for State appropriations to finance the programs for these particular students." Dungan's recommendation struck most board members as impractical for financial, academic, and administrative reasons.

Yet they were fully aware that they were expected to adopt some positive measures. Charles A. Jurgensen, chairman of the Budget and Finance Committee, suggested that the University "set up an experimental program for educationally and economically disadvantaged students by which such students' abilities will be brought up to the standards of the University"; they would then enter the regular academic curricula. President Gross observed that such a commitment would be too extensive and proposed confining admissions to those from Newark, New Brunswick, and Camden high schools.

From these three basic ideas put forward by Dungan, Jurgensen, and Gross, the board moved toward a consensus. Late in the morning, Gustav Heningburg, president of the Greater Newark Urban Coalition, joined the session and made an impassioned plea on behalf of the black students, with whom he had been closely associated during the previous weeks. Rutgers, he urged, must act the role of an urban university; it must become responsive to the realities of Newark. His message impressed the board members.[1]

In the afternoon the governors were ready to act on a statement that reflected the intense and often emotional conference that had gone on for hours behind closed doors. The first paragraph of their statement was taken directly from a document that had been prepared by Gross and Talbott during their negotiations with BOS. It was intended to make the point that Rutgers should not be expected to assume sole responsibility for serving disadvantaged students. It read:

> The University as part of a state-wide system of higher education, which . . . also includes the state colleges and the community colleges, pledges itself to work with these other institutions to the end that every holder of a New Jersey secondary school diploma may find that form of higher education which is best suited to his need, abilities, and aspirations.[2]

Recognizing that a program offering these possibilities did not exist, the board announced its intention to establish

> a new and pioneering program by September, 1969, which initially will open college doors to educationally and economically disadvantaged graduates of the secondary schools in those communities where Rutgers has its primary locations and its most significant community obligations— Newark, New Brunswick, and Camden.

The objective of the program would be to enable such students "to achieve a true Rutgers degree." In time, as funding became available, the University, together with the other institutions in the state system, would "expand the program to the full objective" stated in the first paragraph.

In a fateful final paragraph, the resolution stated that funds would be sought from the legislature to initiate the new program. If such funds were not forthcoming, Rutgers would "fund the program from other sources to insure that it will become a reality in the next academic year." What those "other sources" might be was not readily apparent.[3]

In view of the controversy engendered by this resolution, it is important to analyze what it meant. Although the resolution was mainly designed to meet the demands of protesting blacks, especially those in Newark, it included all educationally and economically disadvantaged students. It did not, strictly speaking, call for an "open admissions" program, for those who entered it would not be fully matriculated students. They would have to take remedial courses and attain an acceptable standard before achieving that status. The greatest impact of the program would be felt in Newark, where the largest black population resided, and secondarily in Camden. The pool from which applicants might come was relatively small in New Brunswick.

The Black Organization of Students received the announcement of the board's action favorably, although they requested some changes in its phrasing. Joe Browne declared it represented "complete agreement with the University on our demands." Bessie Hill, the lone black member of the board, was elated. "I was never more shocked in my life," she exclaimed. "We finally functioned in a way that we should have all along." Although some black spokespersons were more restrained in their reactions, most saw the board's decision as a positive step. The college faculties, which had not been consulted in any way, were stunned and confused; they wondered how the various special programs they had approved earlier would be affected.[4]

70

Around the state, critical comments predominated. President Gross received several hundred letters, two-thirds of them hostile, some even vituperative. The executive committee of the Rutgers Alumni Association condemned the plan, contending it would diminish the value and prestige of a Rutgers diploma. State legislators, who were receiving complaints from irate constituents, expressed their reservations about the board's dramatic proposal.[5]

The critics sounded three main themes. It was wrong for the University to accept hundreds of marginal students when it was turning away even larger numbers of qualified applicants. Rutgers, and especially President Gross, had "caved in" to pressures generated by the illegal and disruptive acts of a small minority. It was highly improper for the board to commit the state to huge and undetermined expenditures without prior legislative approval. For the next several months Gross, and the University Department of Public Relations, campaigned ceaselessly in an effort to address these attacks.

Much would hinge on the stance of the state legislature; realistically it was the only source of funds. The prospects were not encouraging. Greatly disturbed by the building takeovers in Newark and Camden, the legislators early in March had directed Chancellor Dungan to conduct an investigation. He made his report on March 31. It was highly critical of the University. "Black students had cause to be frustrated," he found. "All levels of University faculty and administration bear responsibility for procrastination and for failing to give adequate attention to the need to respond in some manner to student demands." Although he was sympathetic to the black students' grievances, he did not condone disruptive actions, and he called for a statement by all colleges and universities to make it clear that the occupation of buildings would not be tolerated. In one brief sentence the chancellor supported the "experimental program" that he had been instrumental in persuading the Board of Governors to

71

initiate on March 14. The whole tenor of his report was not such as to gain favor for Rutgers with the legislature. Several bills were introduced to impose harsh penalties on students who engaged in disruptions.[6]

The lawmakers were in a critical mood. In April the Education Committees of the two houses asked President Gross to make a written response to twenty-one searching questions. These dealt with every aspect of the recent troubling events, with the internal operations of the University, and with points raised by Dungan in his report. Gross's answers ran to thirty-one single-spaced pages.[7] Still not satisfied and worried by "many critical letters and comments . . . regarding the programs at Rutgers," the two committees held a public hearing on June 9 at which University representatives were grilled about their handling of the black students' demands. It was not a pleasant occasion, especially for President Gross. There were obviously going to be problems in winning support for the new programs. "As I see this entire effort," the director of public relations explained to Gross, "it is a long and difficult task which will get more difficult unless it fails, in which case the consequences will be worse."[8]

Clearly, this was not the time to ask the state for funds to meet the commitments that had been made to the black students. At least until passions subsided, Rutgers would have to look to other sources. By now it was roughly estimated that more than $2 million would be needed. Approaches to foundations were unproductive. Both the Board of Governors and the Board of Trustees maintained small reserve funds that were usually drawn upon only for vital capital expenditures. Seeing no alternative, the two boards agreed to put up $700,000 from these funds to get the new programs started. What would happen if the legislature did not eventually relent and pass a supplemental appropriation was too dreadful to contemplate.[9]

The March 14 resolution of the Board of Governors had

not defined a program; it had merely set forth a policy goal. The huge task of translating the policy into a workable plan was assigned to Assistant Provost John R. Martin. He started from scratch, for there had been no prior thought given to the concept. Without any committee to aid—or hamper—him, Martin consulted widely with many individuals and by April 30 he had devised an elaborate scheme for implementing the boards's vision. It was to be called the Urban University Program (UUP).

Martin's blueprint was imaginative and ambitious.[10] It was based on the principle that each disadvantaged student in the UUP should be provided with a program tailored to his or her individual needs. The students would be offered a range of counseling and support services, along with appropriate developmental courses in areas where they were weak. At the outset they would usually take no more than one regular undergraduate course. Their progress would be carefully monitored by a team of counselor-teachers; when students were deemed to be adequately prepared, they would be recommended for full matriculation. If they were not well adapted to go on, they would be counseled on alternative opportunities in employment or other types of education.

There were five criteria for admissibility to the UUP. Applicants would have to be high school graduates. They would be drawn from families that could afford to contribute less than $625 a year toward their education. They must be unable to meet the normal admission standards. They would be expected to give evidence that they were motivated to seek a college degree. Finally, they must be from the three localities where the University was based. In announcements of the program, Rutgers sources always pointed out that UUP enrollees would not displace any conventionally qualified students; they would be in addition to such students. Moreover, they would not become matriculated until they were prepared to work for "a true

Rutgers degree." Thus the scholarly standards of the University would be maintained.

The actual operation of the UUP would be carried on by Urban University departments in Newark, New Brunswick, and Camden. These units would design and offer developmental courses, provide the student-support teams, and monitor the progress of each student. During the brief period between May and September, about sixty-five teachers, counselors, social workers, psychologists, and other professionals were hastily recruited to staff the three departments. Among them were several undergraduates and recent graduates who had taken active parts in the black student protest movement.[11]

While these preparations were being made, a vigorous recruitment campaign was under way, in which the black student organizations took part. By September 1969, over six hundred UUP students were registered. The majority (369) were in Newark. There were 177 in Camden and only 83 in the New Brunswick colleges. By the second semester slightly more than five hundred remained, and over the summer there was further heavy attrition. Precise data for all three campuses are not available, but it is evident that the great majority of the students—possibly 80 percent—were black, that most had graduated in the bottom half of their high school class, and that males predominated.[12]

Useful as it would be, a full study and appraisal of the UUP is beyond the scope of this narrative. In any event, the program was to be short-lived. Many of the difficulties that soon arose were attributable to the haste with which the UUP was launched. Of even greater import was the awkward status of the three Urban University departments. They were adjuncts to, rather than integrated elements of, the colleges. Their staffs were not members of any faculty. The courses that they offered were not subject to faculty approval and received no college credit. By the same token, the college faculties took a distant, and generally negative, view of the Urban University departments. Indeed, the UUP had the apparent effect of relieving the "regular" faculties of responsibility for the severely disadvantaged students.[13]

The students themselves confronted daunting problems. Most of them were poorly prepared. They could not avoid being aware of their ambiguous position as quasi-members of the student body. Because their stipends covered only their tuition, many had to have jobs in order to maintain themselves and contribute to the support of their families, whose average incomes were below $5,000. The fact that most of their courses earned them no college credits lessened their motivation. Many of their teachers were not well trained for their tasks. When the students were placed in regular college courses, they often floundered.

Newark, with the bulk of the UUP students, faced the greatest challenge. "We were simply not prepared," recalled an original member of the Urban University department there. "We didn't know what we were doing." The Black Organization of Students worked valiantly to make the UUP a success; the members regarded it as "their program." They even ran an off-campus summer orientation session for incoming students in 1969 with funds that they obtained from the Department of Higher Education. Some joined the UUP staff. But their zeal could not overcome all the obstacles. The first head of the program was not a judicious appointment. The department was housed in a building off the main campus. The Newark faculty was committed to its own Special Entrance Program, not to the UUP.[14]

A study made at Newark after three semesters showed that the average UUP student had earned three credits each term. The prediction was that only 10 percent of those who had entered in 1969 would proceed to their degrees. Not until 1972, when the program was reorganized and the Urban University department was replaced by an Academic Foundations department that was incorporated within the college, did

75

conditions improve markedly. Camden went through much the same experience.[15]

Despite the small number of students involved, there were additional complications in New Brunswick. The single Urban University department had to serve UUP students associated with three colleges—Douglass, Rutgers, and the newly opened Livingston College. Each college adopted distinctive procedures for dealing with UUP enrollees, and the result was an administrative nightmare. Livingston, for example, regarded the students as fully matriculated from the start; Douglass and Rutgers evolved their own procedures for determining when a student could be admitted to that status. There were conflicts over who should be responsible for academic advising. The students suffered. Eighty percent of them had graduated in the lower half of their high school class. Eighty-six percent were black. In their first semester they attempted an average of 1.1 credit courses. Only 42 percent received passing grades.[16]

When a noted authority, Dean Allen D. Ballard, Jr., of the City University of New York, was brought in to evaluate the New Brunswick program in the spring of 1971, he underscored what had already become apparent. The "new and pioneering program" was not working well. The basic flaw, as he saw it, lay in the arm's-length relationship between UUP and the colleges. Integration must replace separation. He recommended that teachers have joint appointments, with faculty titles, and that the academic departments become involved in curricular matters affecting UUP students. He also favored greater financial assistance and, where possible, residence on campus. His findings were influential in shaping later developments.[17]

Whether the Urban University Program was ill conceived, or badly managed, whether it was destined to fail as a victim of its detractors, it lasted little more than two years. Chancellor Dungan turned against it. It was a "poorly thought out guilt expiation program," he told a campus reporter. "They took a lot of kids off of the street and shoved them into . . . [UUP]. One should look for black students, or any students for that matter, who can make it."[18] This was not his first salvo against the program. Indeed, almost from the beginning, the Department of Higher Education (DHE) had viewed it critically. DHE had its own program for meeting similar needs—the Educational Opportunity Fund—and the UUP did not come within its guidelines. Before long the University was faced with the choice between maintaining UUP without state funding or following DHE's mandates.

CHAPTER SIX

The Educational Opportunity Fund

*O*UT OF THE TURMOIL ENGENDERED BY the black student protest movement, several distinct programs for disadvantaged undergraduates had taken shape at Rutgers by September 1969. By far the largest was the Urban University Program, initiated on a University-wide basis by the Board of Governors. In addition, there were the several college programs, of which the most fully articulated were those at the Newark College of Arts and Sciences, at Rutgers College, and at Douglass College. Almost unnoticed at the time was yet another venture that had been launched by the Department of Higher Education with modest resources in July 1968. It was known as EOF, the Educational Opportunity Fund. Within three years, after a protracted struggle between the University and DHE, it was to replace all of the Rutgers programs.

This state-sponsored effort to aid educationally and economically disadvantaged high school graduates was, in part, a response to the civil disorders that had ravaged Newark and other New Jersey communities in the summer of 1967. Something

81

had to be done to give hope to young people trapped in urban ghettos. Access to higher education for those victims of poverty and racism might be the answer. In November 1967, Chancellor Dungan sent a memorandum to the presidents of all New Jersey colleges and universities outlining a comprehensive plan for addressing the problem. The response was quite positive. Governor Richard J. Hughes gave his warm endorsement. In May 1968, Assemblyman (later Governor) Thomas H. Kean and ten co-sponsors introduced the necessary legislation, which was enacted in July.[1]

The Educational Opportunity Fund Act was among the first of its kind in the nation. It set forth policies to encourage participating institutions to recruit disadvantaged students, provide them with financial assistance, and offer them appropriate supportive services. These included remedial courses, special counseling, relevant social and cultural activities, and grievance mechanisms. Advisory boards drawn from the community were to assist and monitor the programs. Within the Department of Higher Education, an appointive EOF Board of Directors, chaired by the chancellor, was given broad authority to oversee the management of the program. For the initial year, the legislature appropriated $2 million for EOF; $1,600,000 was for student stipends and $400,000 went to the colleges to assist in financing their support services.[2]

During the academic year 1968–1969, thirty-four New Jersey institutions of higher education participated. Altogether over sixteen hundred EOF students were enrolled, three-fifths of them in the two-year community colleges. Their average stipend was $771, but many were also aided by federal equal opportunity grants, work-study income, and college scholarships. Eighty percent of those enrolled were African Americans; 92 percent came from families with incomes under $7,500. Clearly, EOF was reaching the disadvantaged sector of the state's population. The students, who took both remedial and degree-credit courses, could extend their studies over a period of six years. During the first year there was an attrition rate of only 10 percent, a very encouraging indicator of the success of the program.[3]

Rutgers University had responded affirmatively to Chancellor Dungan's inquiry while EOF was still in the planning stage. When the passage of the enabling legislation seemed assured, DHE invited Rutgers to submit a proposal. In a lengthy response, President Gross outlined the several programs that were already in place at Rutgers and explained that all of them could benefit from additional funding. In essence, he asked for nearly $800,000, half of which would be used to increase the financial packages of disadvantaged students who were already enrolled, or would be by September 1968. The balance would enable Rutgers to take an additional one hundred disadvantaged undergraduates in Newark, three hundred in University College, the evening division, and smaller numbers in the law school and the graduate schools of social work and business.[4]

These proposals were scarcely in line with what DHE had in mind and would have absorbed a large share of EOF's limited resources. In any case, the University received an allotment of only eighty-nine of the more than sixteen hundred EOF grants, or "slots," together with prorated support monies. Perhaps this meager allocation, together with the University's expectation that it could obtain funding for its special programs directly from the legislature, accounts for the scant attention Rutgers administrators gave to EOF in the 1968–1969 academic year.[5]

With the infusion of several hundred disadvantaged students into the University's various special programs in September 1969, confusion quickly arose over the relationship of those programs to EOF. Would these students be eligible for EOF support? The University had received a total of 613 EOF slots for 1969–1970, including 516 for entering students, out of a state-wide total of over four thousand. But because the Rutgers

programs had been instituted without regard for EOF guidelines, it was unclear how the grants would be awared. For
example, under EOF rules, students were expected to be fully
matriculated, yet those enrolled in UUP and in the Rutgers
College TYP did not have that status. Others did not meet the
EOF requirements with regard to family income. A small number were found to be admissible through normal channels, and
therefore were ineligible.

Rutgers College presented the greatest complexities. There
were eighty-nine TYP students and forty-two UUP students.
The former were all housed on the campus, the latter were not;
thus their financial needs were quite different. There was a six-
week summer program for TYP, but not for UUP. Half of the
TYP entrants were not EOF-eligible. The faculty took a proprietary interest in TYP, but not in UUP. In addition, some students who were enrolled neither in TYP nor UUP but were
instead fully matriculated received EOF stipends. It was an in-
credibly confusing administrative, financial, and academic tan-
gle. Fortunately, DHE was lenient in applying EOF guidelines,
thereby easing what could have been an even worse disaster.[6]

From the perspective of Chancellor Dungan and the Department of Higher Education, the situation at Rutgers was
intolerable. There should be but one overall program for disadvantaged students. For Rutgers to anticipate drawing on
EOF to aid some of its students while at the same time it was
planning to ask the legislature to fund programs for other
students made no sense to DHE. Because DHE had the power
to review the University's budget requests, its stance on this
matter was crucial. There were signs as early as November
1969 that DHE intended to wield its authority when it proposed limits on the numbers of students to be admitted to
UUP and TYP. By March 1970, it was insisting that all such
students must meet EOF guidelines.[7]

An early showdown resulted when the University sought a

supplemental appropriation from the legislature to finance its special programs. The $700,000 that had been allocated from reserve funds in June was inadequate, but the temper of the legislature was so hostile that months passed before it was judged to be in a receptive mood. In January 1970, the president of the Senate, Raymond Bateman, sent a confidential aide to Rutgers to study the operation of UUP. He returned with a favorable report. Bateman then introduced a bill to appropriate $747,513 to complete the funding of UUP and TYP for the current year. The measure was speedily approved by the Senate.[8]

It met with quite a different reception in the Assembly, where there continued to be resentment against the Urban University Program and against the way in which Rutgers had initiated it without prior legislative approval. The Republican majority in the lower house recognized that it would be impolitic to deny the requested funds, but it was determined to kill UUP and make Rutgers pay a stiff price for having launched the program. Accordingly, the Assembly voted the $747,513 appropriation, but assigned the money not to Rutgers but to the Eductional Opportunity Fund. The Senate concurred. At the same time, the legislature incorporated in the EOF budget for the next year (1970–1971) the additional funds that would be required to meet the needs of disadvantaged students at Rutgers. The net effect of these actions was to give the Department of Higher Education—through EOF—full control over programs for disadvantaged students at Rutgers.[9]

That was not all. As a further sign of its displeasure, the legislature amended the basic act defining the relationship of Rutgers to the state. This measure tightened the state's fiscal control over the University. No longer could it routinely transfer appropriated monies from one account to another. All accounts were made subject to audit by the state at any time. Further, the University was not to embark on any new ventures that might require state funding without the prior approval of

DHE and the legislature. The lawmakers had made their will known forcefully.[10]

The implications of these legislative actions gradually became clear to University administrators, although it would be some time before they accepted them. Blenda J. Wilson, who was now coordinating all special programs, quickly grasped the central point. "Virtually all of the resources that the University hopes to receive for special programs for disadvantaged students—both financial aid and supportive educational activities—must be received from EOF," she explained to a colleague. This meant that all EOF guidelines would apply. More specifically it meant that inevitably Rutgers would have to abandon its own array of special programs—including UUP—and substitute for them programs that conformed fully to EOF specifications.[11]

For many reasons, this was to be neither an easy nor a congenial task. The University, jealous of its autonomy, was inclined to resent almost any kind of directive from DHE, which in turn was annoyed by the University's apparent recalcitrance. Black students saw in the new trend of events a betrayal of the commitments made to them in 1969, and they protested against the imminent demise of UUP. College faculties were distressed when they were obliged to accept policies mandated by EOF. UUP staff members were unhappy because they foresaw the loss of their positions. Adding to the difficulty was the peculiar organization of the University. Its structure virtually required that there be several college-based EOF programs rather than a unified one for the whole institution.

For a time Rutgers sought to retain its Urban University Program by conforming it to some, though not all, EOF requirements. The new policies were enunciated by Provost Schlatter in December 1970. In the future, UUP students would have to be fully matriculated in a college. They would receive credit for developmental courses, but these credits would not be applicable toward a degree. They would be allowed three semesters to complete fifteen degree-credits in a satisfactory manner. Their class standing would be determined by the number of degree-credits they accumulated. All college deans were directed to take the actions needed to implement these policies. The deans faced a hard assignment in getting their faculties to comply with Schlatter's directive.[12]

These concessions did not satisfy the state EOF board or Chancellor Dungan. Writing to Schlatter in March 1971, Dungan observed that after much correspondence and discussion between his staff and the Rutgers administration "we are no closer to resolving our problems than we were a year ago." He expressed "serious misgivings" about the high attrition rate and excessive costs of the Urban University Program. He was critical of the apparent duplication of effort in providing supportive services for the Special Entrance Program at Newark and the Transitional Year Program at Rutgers as well as for UUP. Schlatter attempted to address Dungan's specific concerns. He added that he was awaiting the report of an outside consultant (Dean Ballard) on UUP and that, at the request of the Board of Governors, he was appointing a high-level committee to recommend modifications in Rutgers's programs for disadvantaged students.[13]

The unequal tug-of-war continued. In April, DHE announced flatly, ". . . we are not funding the Urban University Department at Rutgers." All UUP students must be "brought into the ongoing EOF programs of the various colleges." Furthermore, EOF was "not to be administered as a modified open admission's program." The meaning and force of these statements were unmistakable. Rutgers had to capitulate.[14]

In June 1971, the two parties reached an understanding. Rutgers agreed to consolidate its special programs on the EOF model. Teachers of remedial courses would be granted full faculty status. Admissions requirements would be tightened somewhat and students would have to register for at least six degree-credits each semester. They would be fully matriculated and receive the same letter of admission as "regular" students. The college Scholastic Standing Committees would evaluate the records of EOF students on the same basis as all other students. No longer would Rutgers give a geographical preference to disadvantaged applicants from Newark, New Brunswick, and Camden. All of these changes were to be effected by July 1, 1972.[15]

Meanwhile an Ad Hoc Committee on Special Programs, headed by Dean Milton Schwebel of the Graduate School of Education, was wrestling with the problem of how to make the transition to the new order. It held twelve meetings over a ten-month period. Contention within the committee centered around the issue of replacing the New Brunswick–wide Urban University Department by Academic Foundation departments within each college and granting faculty status to members of those departments, as directed by DHE. When black students protested because they were not represented on the committee, several of them were added. The deans of Rutgers College and Douglass College opposed the creation of Academic Foundations departments in their units. By the time the committee reported, its recommendations were all but irrelevant. Most of the essential changes mandated by DHE had already been made by the central administration.[16]

Under the new arrangements, each undergraduate college had its own EOF program, with its own director, budget, and staff. EOF directors reported to their college deans. An administrator at the University level attempted to coordinate the dealings of the college programs with the state EOF office. At the Newark College of Arts and Sciences, Livingston College, and Rutgers-Camden, remedial instruction and counseling services were organized in Academic Foundation departments, which were integrated into the structure of the colleges. Douglass College and Rutgers College did not fully adopt this model;

they relied instead on the existing academic departments for remedial courses. In time, other undergraduate units also added EOF programs. This multiplicity of college-based programs, together with the weak authority of the University EOF administrator, had many advantages, but it frequently occasioned confusion for DHE.[17]

By September 1972, then, UUP and such special college programs as TYP and SEP had all given way to EOF. The University had resisted the transformation, and black students had opposed aspects of the new order. But the state controlled the essential financial resources and could not be balked. Fortunately, state-wide funding for EOF rose steeply after 1968; from $2 million in that year to $16 million by 1976. Thus it was possible for Rutgers to enroll over two thousand disadvantaged students—two thirds of them black—in the latter year. If the full potentialities of this program could have been foreseen when it was first established, both the thrust of the black student protest movement and the University's response to it might have been quite different. On the other hand, the protests, and the University's commitment as expressed so conspicuously in the Urban University Program, undoubtedly spurred the rapid expansion of EOF.

Cataclysmic social changes are never orderly; neither do they follow a predictable course. The Rutgers experience illustrates this truism. Starting in 1965, largely in response to recently enacted federal civil rights legislation, University authorities had begun to plan for increased minority enrollments. These efforts were guided by the Council on Equal Opportunity, and produced modest results. Then came the demands and protests by black students on all campuses in February 1969. In New Brunswick and Camden, college faculties attempted to respond by creating a variety of special programs. Different conditions maintained in Newark, where protracted negotiations between the Black Organization of Students and administrative officers

89

failed to produce an agreement acceptable to all parties, including the faculty. At that point the Board of Governors assumed the initiative and set forth the policy that brought the Urban University Program into being. Meanwhile, almost unnoticed amidst the turmoil, the state's newly created Educational Opportunity Program had appeared on the scene.

Almost inevitably, a period of confusion ensued. The college programs, UUP, and EOF each had their champions. Each reflected the diverse orientations of their sponsors—the college faculties, the Board of Governors, and the Department of Higher Education—and represented three different kinds of responses to the same challenge. The college programs were the least innovative; the faculties tended to be cautious in setting aside traditional procedures and values. The Urban University Program was the most daring, in that it imposed virtually no conventional admission requirements and undertook a vast remediation effort through the Urban University departments. The Educational Opportunity Fund occupied what can be characterized as a middle position. Its guidelines were more liberal than those of the college programs but more stringent than those of UUP. Ultimately, of course, EOF prevailed, not as a consequence of deliberate choice by the college faculties or the Board of Governors but because of the external authority wielded by the Department of Higher Education.

CHAPTER SEVEN

Postscript

*T*HE VARIED INITIATIVES THAT RESULTED FROM the black student protest movement of 1969 affected every dimension of Rutgers University. Perhaps the most obvious consequence was that five years later there were over twenty-five hundred black full-time undergraduates, slightly more than 10 percent of the total student enrollment. In addition, nearly one thousand African American men and women attended the several graduate and professional schools, and eleven hundred were registered in the evening divisions of the University. Blacks constituted approximately 5 percent of the full-time faculty and made up a larger proportion of the non-academic work force. In terms of sheer numbers, change had come rapidly.[1]

Other outcomes, though less susceptible to quantification, were no less significant. Black and Hispanic recruiters were added to the staffs of all the admissions offices to stimulate applications from minority candidates. Financial aid administrators, similarly reinforced, served a new and burgeoning clientele. Delicate issues were raised regarding on-campus housing, especially when minority groups sought to segregate themselves in certain dormitory sections. Black student organizations proliferated and contended for their fair share of funds to support their activities. Soon there was a newspaper (*Black Voice*) and black fraternities and sororities.

In direct response to student pressures, new courses were included in the curriculum. Within a year or two, college faculties approved majors in African American studies, and in some colleges the field acquired departmental status. In like manner, an impetus was given to urban studies, African languages, and special programs for those preparing to teach in urban schools. Not least of all, there were six-week summer sessions to provide an introduction to college-level work and a wide array of remedial courses offered either by Academic Foundation departments or by the established disciplines. As the various programs yielded to EOF guidelines after 1972, each college had an EOF staff to counsel and support the students who were funded from that source. In quite a different area, the University's athletic teams—which had been overwhelmingly white prior to 1969—now featured large numbers of black men and women.

Livingston College was something of a special case. This new undergraduate college, located across the Raritan River from New Brunswick on the site of the former Camp Kilmer, opened with its first contingent of seven hundred students in September 1969. Its planners had determined that it would be an experimental college, breaking with many conventional practices. The college made exceptional efforts to recruit "nontraditional" and minority students and oriented its curriculum toward such contemporary problems as racism and urbanization. A distinctive grading system, the awarding of academic credit for "life experience," a heavy emphasis on community internships, and considerable flexibility in the design of individual student programs set Livingston apart from the other colleges in New Brunswick. So too did its system of internal governance, which involved full student participation and representation based on racial apportionment.

When Livingston opened, about a quarter of its student body and a fifth of its faculty were black or Puerto Rican. By 1974, those groups comprised 30 percent of the college's total enrollment of 3,342, a much higher percentage than in the other undergraduate units. At least in its early years, Livingston was regarded by minority students as "their" college. By the same token, this image did not serve it well in its relations with the older colleges or with large segments of the public. In 1971, following a series of highly publicized incidents of internal disorder, some of them reflective of racial tensions, an investigative panel recommended that the administrative structure of the college be strengthened and that the faculty assume a larger role in decisions related to student life. In time the aggressively experimental character of Livingston moderated, but it continued to be distinguished by its special commitment to minority students.[2]

Clearly, great changes had been wrought at Rutgers as a consequence of the 1969 protests. But the black student protest movement did not end with that year; it remained a lively force through the ensuing decade. As their numbers swelled, African American students were aggrieved by the conditions that they confronted at Rutgers. Their complaints were directed against both old and new targets: the insensitivity of the campus police, the paucity of appealing cultural activities, the bureaucracy of the financial aid offices, the high attrition rate, the scarcity of black faculty, and the inadequacy of academic support programs.

More fundamental was their sense that their presence at Rutgers was at best tolerated, and more commonly resented. Scrawled racial epithets, hostile stares, and overbearing attitudes reminded them constantly of their alien status. Except in such sports as football, basketball, and track they took little part in predominantly white campus organizations. Instead, through their own fraternities, sororities, political and cultural organizations, and living groups they sought to create for themselves a separate and protective environment.

Throughout the decade after 1969, a spirit of militancy continued to animate black students.[3] They employed rhetoric and tactics that were reminiscent of 1969; they organized mass demonstrations accompanied by the presentation of lists of demands. They did not, however, generate the sense of urgency and crisis that had distinguished the events of 1969, nor did the University authorities react with the same immediacy. A brief look at some of the more prominent incidents may serve to illustrate the atmosphere that prevailed.[4]

There were several organized protests in 1971, the most turbulent of which was at Camden. That campus was thrown into turmoil in mid-February by rallies, demonstrations, bomb scares, and vandalism, and the discord persisted into May. Discontent first surfaced when black students complained about the high rate of attrition in the Urban University Program. Soon other grievances were voiced; many of them centered around the need to improve the structure, staffing, and curriculum of the Urban University Program. There was also a demand that the college have 50 percent black and Puerto Rican enrollment by September 1972.

As the faculty sought to address some of these issues, racial tensions were raised by the dismissal of a popular black UUP instructor, Roy Jones, who had been one of the student leaders of BSUM in 1969. Demonstrations and strike calls culminated early in April with the vandalization of the college library, which led to the jailing of several students and more protests. With the end of the term, the furor subsided. Meanwhile, the dean and faculty, although limited by the available resources, struggled to meet the legitimate criticisms that had been directed against the Urban University Program.[5]

At Rutgers College in March 1971, over three hundred black students signed a petition demanding of the dean and the Board of Governors that an autonomous department of African American studies be established. To underscore their insistence, about two hundred and fifty protesters threw down their food trays, smashed china, and overturned tables and chairs in the main dining hall. Plans for the creation of the new department were already well advanced; the Department of Africana Studies was in operation with the start of the new academic year.[6]

Although there were no overt demonstrations at Douglass College, friction between black and white students, involving mutual charges of harrassment, belligerent behavior, and exclusiveness occasioned the appointment of a Commission on Ethnic and Race Relations in April 1971. During the course of nine hearings, the commission learned of many "incidents" of interracial clashes. White students viewed blacks as disruptive aggressors; blacks saw whites as insensitive and domineering. The commission's recommendations called on both groups to exercise more tolerance and understanding. Whites, in particular, should not be offended by what they regarded as "black separatism"; blacks in turn should recognize that "the establishment of a completely separate and viable black community within the larger Douglass community is not a realistic goal."[7]

An accumulation of unresolved issues eventuated in several demonstrations involving hundreds of African American students from all the undergraduate colleges in New Brunswick in 1973. On November 5 about one hundred protesters occupied the second floor of the administration building at Livingston College for over eight hours. They issued a list of forty-two demands, calling for the removal of the dean of student affairs, the reorganization of that office to better serve black students, the relaxation of security regulations, the opening of the campus to the outside community, and the improvement of health services. After the building had been evacuated, President Edward J. Bloustein met with representatives of the protesters, agreed to act at once on some of their demands, and asked the acting dean of the college to appoint a task force to study and report on the other items.[8]

A few days later nearly three hundred and fifty black students from Livingston, Rutgers, and Douglass appeared before the Board of Governors to ask for immediate action on their grievances. The Livingston representatives reiterated their previous demands. The Douglass students sought a liberalization of the grading system, larger representation on the student academic affairs committee, and a review of the college's admissions policy. Rutgers College black students, who had charged the college with institutional racism the previous December, complained about the lack of action on their demands for reforms.

Further to express their concern about the failure of the University to undertake prompt redress of their grievances, black students disrupted a basketball game, engaged in massive withdrawals of books from the college libraries, and staged a noisy march through the Administrative Services Building. Meanwhile, a Select Committee to Study the Issue of Rutgers College as a Multi-Racial Community—headed by Professor Warren Susman—found that the college and the University had failed to live up to its commitments to minority students and unanimously endorsed the substance of their complaints.[9]

The University's response to the wide array of grievances that had been expressed was summarized by President Bloustein in a widely distributed report, "Promises to Keep," in May 1974. He first pointed out the progress that had been made since 1969. Rutgers ranked fourth among all public universities in its proportion of black students. The retention rate over a one-year period for students in EOF programs was 65 percent, as compared with the comparable rate of 75 percent for "regular" students. Two-thirds of EOF students were black. Vigorous affirmative action procedures were bringing more blacks to the faculty at tenured ranks. A recent University-wide salary review had resulted in adjustments for minority faculty.

But the president went on to acknowledge that renewed efforts were needed, especially with regard to financial aid, counseling, record keeping, supportive academic services, and admissions policies. Then he described the steps that were being taken to address these problem areas. The University, he insisted, must "re-invigorate its special efforts to bring minority students into the University and help them attain degrees." Once again, strongly supported demonstrations, some of them disruptive, had been effective in gaining the attention of the University's authorities and eliciting positive responses.[10]

For the next few years racial issues were relatively muted, whether because of the corrective actions that had been taken or because of a decline in militancy among black students. By 1979 black full-time undergraduates numbered 3,303, an all-time high that was not to be exceeded in the following decade. The largest number (866) were enrolled in Livingston College, and blacks exceeded 10 percent of the enrollments at the Newark College of Arts and Sciences (634), Rutgers College (631), Douglass College (391), and the Camden College of Arts and Sciences (395). For all divisions of the University, they constituted 11.6 percent of the total of over forty-nine thousand students. Only three other public universities—City University of New York, Wayne State, and Temple—had higher proportions.

These impressive statistics did not mean that all was well at Rutgers. Indeed, 1979 brought a renewal of protests comparable to those of 1971 and 1973. They were centered on the New Brunswick campuses, where a coalition of black student organizations again levelled complaints against familiar targets: recruitment and admissions policies, financial aid awards, the small number of black faculty, "racist harassment," the inequitable allocation of student activity fees, and high rates of attrition.

Although many concerns animated the protests, perhaps the most fundamental one had to do with "academic success," or rate of graduation. Black students were being enrolled in record numbers, but too few were receiving degrees.[11]

The first reliable study of graduation rates was made in 1979. It did not distinguish among students on the basis of race, but it did compare the performance of EOF-funded students with non-EOF students. Over 60 percent of those in the first categroy were black. The study reported that while 62 percent of the non-EOF students who had entered in 1973 graduated in five years, only 27 percent of EOF students received their degrees within the same period. Obviously, this discrepancy was cause for concern.[12]

On April 12, a day after presenting their demands, hundreds of minority students marched to President Bloustein's office to express their outrage. He assured them that they would receive a preliminary reply a week later, after the New Brunswick provost and college committees had an opportunity to consider and respond to the grievances. On April 19 the president was confronted by over five hundred black students as he released a fourteen-page report that recited the University's record in serving minority students and reported actions that were being taken to meet some of the demands. Others would require further study. He asked that a small delegation of students assist in this process. His remarks were not well received, and the demonstrators marched across the city to Douglass College.[13]

A few weeks later President Bloustein reported to the Board of Governors on the recent incidents. He acknowledged that supportive services for special students were inadequate, despite the fact that the University provided $1,400,000 from its own funds to supplement the resources provided by the state from the Educational Opportunity Fund. He then appointed a task force, headed by Vice-President Paul G. Pearson, which

100

worked through the summer to produce a comprehensive response to the eleven demands.[14]

Pearson's report was issued in September. It observed that although efforts had been made to establish a "constructive dialogue" with black student leaders, "these attempts were met only by confrontation and subsequently by silence." Nevertheless, the administration had taken several actions. To improve the handling of financial aid, five financial aid service centers were conveniently located on the several campuses. The Graduate School was recruiting minority students who would now be eligible for funding from federal sources. Seven additional positions had been made available for basic skills and counseling programs. Efforts were under way to improve cultural and social activities for minority students. Two staff positions had been added to the Office of Career Counseling and Placement to serve minority job seekers. A Minority Faculty Research Development Program would be instituted to enable more such faculty to qualify for tenure. Other sections of the report defended the University's policies on such matters as recruitment, admissions, security, and faculty development. The report concluded with a warning that demonstrators who disrupted the normal business of the academic community would be subject to disciplinary action. No direct mention was made of attrition rates, although various commitments were made to enhance basic skills training.[15]

Leaders of the Black Student Congress told the Board of Governors that this response was unacceptable. It did not adequately address the concerns of their constituents about their prospects for academic survival. Consequently, they continued to exert pressure. In February 1980, there was another highly publicized disruption of a basketball game, which resulted in five arrests. Displeased with *Targum*'s coverage of the incident, irate blacks burned fifteen hundred copies of the student paper and invaded its editorial offices. There was another massive check-out of books from the library.[16]

These tactics were not ineffectual. Even though they alienated many white students—and the editors of *Targum*—they induced the central administration and the Board of Governors to study the complaints that were being voiced. In particular, they created a heightened awareness of the importance of addressing the issues of retention and graduation rates.

This new emphasis was evident in updated progress reports issued by the New Brunswick provost in 1980 and 1981. These stressed improvements that were being made in academic support programs and in all the related areas that impinged on the ability of black students to survive at the University. Efforts were under way in each collegiate unit to "integrate minority students more fully into campus life and to increase the sensitivity of predominantly white student organizations to the needs and interests of minority students."[17]

Thus the decade of the 1970s saw a continuation of the black student protest movement at Rutgers; militancy did not end with the events of 1969. Oddly enough, only the Newark campus, the most conspicuous theater of controversy in 1969, had no major upheavels. The main arena was New Brunswick. There the protests followed a fairly consistent pattern. Coalitions of black student organizations would formulate demands, which varied little from year to year. They would then stage demonstrations, typically climaxed by a march on the president's office. Further to show their anger, they engaged in such disruptive actions as occupying buildings, upsetting library routines, halting basketball games, invading administrative offices, and the like. These actions tended to offend the white majority and to invoke at least the threat of disciplinary sanctions.

There also came to be a patterned response by the University authorities. Because it was usually the main target, the central administration was called upon to formulate a response to the demands, and to do so within an impossibly brief period of time. Some preliminary statement would be made, the Board of Governors would become involved, and various agencies would be created—or designated—to investigate grievances and come up with recommendations for corrective actions. Rarely was there any prolonged or meaningful dialogue with representatives of the black student organizations. The process would conclude with a lengthy statement, or report, which pointed to the progress that had been achieved since 1969, conceded that more had to be accomplished, and described new initiatives that would be taken to meet obvious problems. Faculty bodies played little role in the process. In most instances they were bypassed both by the protesters and by the central administration.

Each protest, then, brought forth positive responses. This is not to say that every perceived grievance was addressed, or that the new measures quieted the suspicions and anxieties of the protesters. Quite the contrary; the issues involved could not all be resolved so readily. The long-established academic structure was not inflexible, but the values, orientations, and procedures that lay at its core were resistant to radical transformation. And the University could not be detached from the larger society, where ingrained racial attitudes had still to be reckoned with. There was another difficulty. Even with the strongest possible commitment on the part of all who were involved, the answer to the question of what was required to move beyond equality of access to a higher goal of equality of achievement remained elusive.

The decade of the 1970s had brought unprecedented numbers of blacks into what had formerly been predominantly white colleges and universities. The Rutgers experience was not atypical in this regard. But this progress was not sustained in the 1980s, for reasons that are still the subject of study and controversy. In New Jersey, while the numbers of black high school graduates remained relatively stable, the proportion

103

going on to post-secondary education fell. Between 1978 and 1985, black enrollments in four-year institutions declined by 12 percent; at the two-year community colleges the comparable figure was 32 percent. Over the same years the drop at Rutgers was 17 percent. The falling rate of college attendance was especially severe among black males. Statewide, and at Rutgers, the proportion of EOF-funded students who were black changed drastically. Whereas they had comprised 60 percent of EOF students at Rutgers in 1977, that proportion fell to 43 percent by 1987. Approximately 60 percent of those students were women.

No less disheartening were the statistics measuring progress toward degrees. State-wide in 1985 blacks accounted for 12 percent of college enrollments but received only 7 percent of bachelor's degrees. The picture was more favorable at Rutgers, where blacks in 1985 comprised 9 percent of the full-time undergraduates and received over 7 percent of the degrees awarded. But whereas nearly two-thirds of all undergraduates who entered in 1979 graduated within six years, fewer than half of black entrants achieved that goal.[18]

The steady decline in black enrollments did not, as might have been expected, lead to student protests. Throughout the 1980s, the customary signs of black militancy were not apparent; there were no mass demonstrations such as those that had erupted in the previous decade. Now pressure on the University to recruit more minority students came from a different source, the New Jersey Department of Higher Education.

In March 1986, Chancellor T. Edward Hollander sent a powerful, well-documented memorandum to the Board of Higher Education.[19] It described the reversal of the trends that had seemed so promising in the 1970s and set forth a multifaceted program to boost minority enrollments. His recommendations were speedily adopted. Several of them had a direct impact on Rutgers.

The University was required to establish a "permanent working group" to draft a "strategic plan to address declining minority enrollments," implement the plan, and make periodic progress reports to the Department of Higher Education. To meet a related directive, the Board of Governors in April created an Ad Hoc Committee on Minority Recruitment and Retention, which monitored new initiatives. DHE also decreed that college EOF programs that did not enroll 10 percent of incoming freshmen would be placed on probation and receive no increase in funding while in that status. Five of the fifteen undergraduate units at Rutgers were affected by this policy.

The University had not been indifferent to the drop in minority enrollments, but Hollander's directives energized the Board of Governors, the central administration, and subordinate agencies. Within a year, the number of students receiving EOF awards began to climb. But there was no appreciable increase in the number of black full-time undergraduates because they made up a declining proportion of the EOF category. More productive were special merit scholarships for outstanding African American and Puerto Rican high school graduates. Named for James Dickson Carr, Rutgers's first black graduate, they were instituted in 1986 and carried generous stipends. Other special scholarships gave financial recognition to minority undergraduates who did not quality for EOF assistance. There were also more sophisticated recruitment campaigns, targeted at different segments of the pool of potential candidates. Complementing these endeavors were additional resources for supportive academic services. Altogether, the University's response to the issues raised by Chancellor Hollander signalized yet another phase of its ongoing efforts to cope with a continuing challenge.[20]

During the academic year 1988–1989, Rutgers commemorated the twentieth anniversaries of the Educational Opportunity Fund and the 1969 protests. Under the rubric "Challenge

105

'69: Retrospect and New Visions," several events were staged that focused attention on the role of minorities within the University. It was an appropriate time to attempt an overview of the changes that had occurred and to consider what lay ahead. Many of those who had been activist leaders in 1969, now established in remarkably successful careers, participated in the programs. They were duly, if belatedly, recognized for their courageous and effective actions.[21]

Rutgers had indeed experienced great changes since the occupation of Conklin Hall, but there was a general sense that the time had not yet arrived to celebrate the successful completion of a mission. The proportion of "historically underrepresented" minorities (blacks, Puerto Ricans, Hispanics) in 1988 stood at 17 percent of full-time undergraduates. Adding in the Asian category brought the minority fraction to over 25 percent. Rutgers, once predominantly white, had become a multiracial community. But blacks comprised only 10 percent of the student body, close to the mark that had been attained by 1975. Similarly, black representation in the graduate divisions and on the full-time faculty hovered near the 1975 level of 5 percent. In the face of adverse nation-wide trends, Rutgers was struggling to maintain black enrollments and black faculty.[22]

The picture was not much brighter with respect to rates of attrition. Throughout the 1980s, those rates remained remarkably constant. One-fifth of blacks did not survive beyond the first year; fewer than half were still enrolled after four years. After six years, about 45 percent had rececived degrees. (For all students, the comparable rate was around 65 percent.) There were considerable variations among colleges. At the older, more selective residential units in New Brunswick three-fifths of black students graduated within six years, while in the urban colleges at Camden and Newark the proportion was closer to one-fourth.[23]

106

As these disconcerting indicators of academic achievement came under scrutiny after 1986, there were redoubled efforts to reduce attrition rates. Every college restructured and augmented its basic skills courses. In New Brunswick, a "Gateway Program" provided special sections of introductory courses to students in need of remediation, with encouraging early results. An Office of Minority Undergraduate Science Programs sponsored several programs to both recruit and prepare students who might seek careers in science or medicine. Newark had a Retention Project, with funding from the Department of Higher Education; Camden introduced a "Learning to Learn" course. Several symposia, organized by the assistant vice-president for academic affairs–retention, brought together faculty members, counselors, and administrators to exchange ideas on how best to enhance retention efforts. By 1989 there were some eighty programs or agencies specifically committed to serving minority students at all levels of the University. How effective they will be has yet to be determined.[24]

How best to summarize the twenty-year record? We might recall that down to 1969, Rutgers had no more than four hundred black graduates. Since that year, some seven thousand African American men and women have been awarded baccalaureate degrees; over twenty-five hundred have earned advanced degrees. In 1968, there were but one hundred black lawyers in New Jersey. The Rutgers Law School, through its pioneering Minority Student Program, was responsible for more than doubling that number within a decade; by 1988 it counted 854 graduates, most of them black.

These raw facts can scarcely suggest what such achievements represent in terms of struggles against adversity, of personal growth and satisfaction, or enriched human contributions to our society. They barely imply the awful costs of the policies of exclusion that prevailed before minority youth could develop

107

their talents through access to higher education. Today, the conditions that confront black schoolchildren, especially in urban areas, are even worse than those that inspired the 1969 protests. The challenge so well defined at that time still confronts us. To meet it will require more in the way of commitment, resources, and ingenuity than have been evidenced over the past twenty years.

APPENDIXES

Appendix I

Grievances and Demands Presented by New Brunswick Black students to the Board of Governors, April 19, 1968

Grossly inadequate number of Black Students attending the State University.

Inadequate number of Black Deans and Black Administration Personnel.

A need for an Afro-American Studies Department.

A need for the institution of Black Culture, Music, and Literature.

Greater variety of literature of contemporary Black Authors in the University Library and Book Store, as well as the Student Centers.

Demand investigation of Campus Patrol, specifically, discriminatory practices.

Creation of Financial Committee to provide financial and scholarship aid to Black Students. (It is intended that this committee consist of some Black as well as white members.)

Inadequate dissemination of information regarding tutorial programs. Follow-up Program—Adjust workload similar to program operating at Douglass.

Re-evaluation of grading system.

Permit creation of Black Dormitory section.

Recognition of Black Alumni, i.e., restoration of Paul Robeson to all privileges and immunities.

In commemoration of the Noblest black Son of Rutgers, name the Student Center "Paul Robeson Student Center."

Permit creation of Black Fraternity consonant with state and university rules and regulations.

Permanent committee of administration and Black Students to create dialogue and communication.

Proposals Presented to Board of Governors by the Black Organiza-tion of Students (Newark), April 19, 1968

The Black Organization of Students at Rutgers-Newark was dismayed when we received no formal reply to our communica-tion dated March 5, concerning our request to appear before the Board of Governors. I have a copy of that letter with me. Instead we were informed by word of mouth to the effect that we would have to go through channels to approach the Board of Governors. This action we undertook. Subsequently, we at Rutgers-Newark learned this bureaucratic process was elimi-nated for the New Brunswick group when the University was subjected to a verbal attack. We can draw no other conclusion than that Rutgers-Newark, like black Americans today, enjoys second-class citizenship in the Rutgers family; and that peti-tions originating at Rutgers-Newark receive all too often a casual perusal and paternalistic toleration.

Therefore, our first proposal as citizens of Rutgers attending classes in Newark is that the perennial, black sheep image, which falsely characterizes Rutgers-Newark as a group of build-ings that serve as stopover sites for dim-witted, apathetic, poverty-stricken high school graduates, be dispelled. We main-tain that Rutgers-Newark be allowed to assume her responsibil-ity and be accorded her proper recognition. We may lack the grassy knolls of other divisions of Rutgers, but the keen minds, concern for community, and a sense of present-day reality we do fully possess.

Our second proposal is that the University begin to actively recruit and secure more black students from Newark and the surrounding areas. As of today, April 19, 1968, the full-time black student population attending day school at Rutgers-Newark is approximately 2% of the total student enrollment. Numerically, this may be expressed as 62 black students out of the 3,050 total student body. We also urge the use of black

113

students on any committee that will concern itself with the proposed recruitment.

Our third proposal is that the University establish at Rutgers-Newark a department of Urban Affairs with special emphasis on the black community and its changing role within the urban complex. This is manditory if Rutgers-Newark is to become a functional part of the community in which it is located.

Our fourth proposal is that the University establish a department of Urban Education at the graduate level. This would fill the vacuum created by a lack of proper emphasis in existing teacher preparation as it relates to urban teaching situations. The need for such a program manifests itself in the despairing mockery of the educational process that is evident in Newark's school system.

Our fifth proposal is that The John Cotton Dana Library establish a separate reading room which would contain books and other materials written by and dealing with black people. At present, our library has a marked deficiency in the aforementioned material. With a growing awareness of black contributions to the American society, it would appear that Rutgers-Newark would deem it imperative that this situation is rectified.

Our sixth proposal is that the University see fit to establish a Department of African Affairs. Its purpose would be to dispel the all pervasive charicature of Africa as the home of savages who may occasionally be enlightened by sarfaris of benevolent whites. This department could also serve to bring to light the effect of African contributions, both past and present, on world cultures.

Our seventh proposal is that the University develop a sensitivity to the needs of the community in which it is located, and that it begin to service these needs. B.O.S. has suggested, for a start, that beginning September 1968, Rutgers-Newark institute an inter-disciplinary seminar on the problems of and possible solutions to what is now termed the black ghetto in Newark.

Our eighth proposal is that the University begin to actively seek and by this means employ black persons for faculty positions. We, in Newark, are appalled by the fact that not one member of our faculty is black. Attention should also be given to the use of black graduate school students at Rutgers-Newark. They too are completely lacking.

Our ninth proposal is that the University establish a scholarship fund that would provide funds for a number of high school students from the Newark metropolitan area. We also propose that this scholarship be designated for a student who has the intention of attending Rutgers-Newark.

Appendix III

The continuing policy of BOS is that there can be no changes in the total enrollment at Rutgers-Newark without substantial changes in the attitudes of this institution. Specifically, a transformation of Rutgers University must occur. Pro-white nationalism and racism must be replaced by a sensitivity and responsiveness that will be representative of the University's total constituency. Such measures must be enacted through the restructuring of existing policies, programs, and curricula which must be expressly designed to meet the desires and needs of Blacks. Thus, we will be insured of the adequate preparation necessary to undertake the task of improving the lot of our people by determining our own destiny.

In line with this position, it is the conclusion of the BOS that any changes in the University's admissions policies MUST be accompanied by innovations in other areas of the University. These innovations dictate:

- I. That an immediate review of the entire Rutgers-Newark admissions department be made to accertain the reason for the general decline in the number of enrollees and specifically the number of Black enrollees;
    - a. That BOS members be included in this committee of review;
        - (1) That as members of the University's constituency, Black students have a right to be a part of this committee;
    - b. That there be an immediate removal of admissions director, Robert Swab, and his assistant, C. T. Miller;

(1) Admissions figures announced by Mr. Swab reveal his inefficiencies as admissions director;

(2) Mr. Swab has failed to sufficiently comb Black high schools for applicants from ghetto areas;

(3) The attitudes of Mr. Swab and Mr. Miller are basically prejudiced as is evidenced by their refusals to implement sincere programs to channel Black students;

(4) Mr. Miller's biased attitude has been made apparent through his tendencies to be extremely hostile, derogatory and arrogant in dealing with Black applicants;

II. That Black students be employed on a work-study basis in the admissions office to implement the recruitment of Black students;

    a. Recent policies have encouraged off-campus work-study jobs in the community;

III. That there be an immediate creation of two salary-lines providing for the hiring of two Black administrators to work specifically in the area of Black student recruitment;

    a. That a fund be provided for these administrators and BOS to use in setting up programs for high school Blacks;

        (1) Existing programs are irrelevant to the vast majority of Blacks;

        (2) These new programs would take the University to the potential student as well as take the potential student to the University;

        (3) This demand is not unprecedented

117

in that other major institutions have used this method to gain a greater percentage of Black students;

b. That these Black administrators must have the approval of the Black Organization of Students;

    (1) To insure that these administrators will be free of University attempts to appease Black students, this demand is made to assure that the persons chosen will be ones of understanding, sensitivity, and responsiveness to Black needs and desires;

c. That these administrators shall have a dual function;

    (1) That they will be able to increase the Black student enrollment;

        (a) The programs and actions of these administrators will be made relevant to Black applicants;

    (2) That they will be able to improve Rutgers-Newark and community relations;

        (a) By correcting community impressions of the University, these administrators will be able to improve community involvement and aid in recruiting Black students;

IV. Consistent with previous positions taken by BOS regarding the admission of Black students, the proportion of full-time Black students enrolled over the next two or three years must be commensurate with the total population of Newark and its surrounding communities. Irrefutable evidence that Rutgers-Newark is attempting to achieve this goal must be shown in admissions figures for the 1969–70 academic year. For example, we strongly advocate that these figures should represent no less than 30% of the total enrollment. (This figure should not be interpreted as suggestive of a quota.)

    a. Due to past discriminatory policies exercised by the University against Black people, this position constitutes a *minimal* degree of *justifiable* "restitution";

V. Remedial, tutorial, and other special compensatory programs initiated during the 1968–69 academic year must be expanded and broadened;

VI. That a special scholarship be established for the use of Black students who fulfill the academic requirements of Rutgers-Newark, but lack the financial resources;

    a. It is the opinion of BOS that if the University is sincere in its efforts to bring qualified Blacks into this institution, Rutgers-Newark will act to establish funds for academically qualified applicants;

    b. Although funds are available for so called risk students, there are no funds allocated specifically for non-risk students;

VII. That a committee including Black representatives be created to formulate new admissions criteria;

VIII. That there will be a Black officer hired in the Dean of Students office;

    a. That this officer must meet the approval of the Black Organization of Students;

        (1) Although a salary-line for this officer has been allowed for in the present budget proposals, we feel that

119

our approval is mandatory to guard against the hiring of an insensitive Black person;

IX. That monies be made available to the Black Organization of Students for the specific purpose of planning and developing community and campus projects;

    a. A precedent for such action has already been established within the University in the form of allocations to RSVP. Although RSVP has been instituted to bring about student-community involvement, the Black Organization of Students feels that we can better serve our community as residents of this community by formulating self-help projects that can project the ideal of Black esteem;

X. That an active policy of recruitment and hiring of Black academic and advisory staff be at least proportionate to the total number of Black students and consistent with the demand outlined in section IV;

    a. It is the consensus of the Black Organization of Students that this demand is justified by the realization that people of similar backgrounds and attitudes identify more readily;

    b. Black students would be able to relate to Black advisors with greater ease and because of the similarity of interests and backgrounds, the advisors could more realistically comprehend Black student needs and desires;

XI. There there will be developed a comprehensive Black Studies Institute WITH degree-granting status and a full-time coordinator;

    a. One reason for the lack of interest in R-N as a primary college choice is the lack of identification materials for Blacks on this campus;

    b. This Black Studies Institute will provide a

needed element of Black identification on campus;

c. This institute, located on Newark, would serve to attract Blacks interested in pursuing the field of Black studies as a possible career choice.

Appendix IV

1. We demand more Black students on the Rutgers, New Brunswick campus. At present there is a miniscule percentage of Black students in proportion to the total population—1.7% (95 Black students out of a student body of 6,400).

   We demand that the number of Black students be increased to 11% of the total population of Rutgers College in order to reflect the percentage of the Black population in the state of New Jersey. In order to enroll more Black students on the Rutgers College (New Brunswick) campus, there must be a change in the policy of admissions, so as to permit the following:

   We demand that all New Jersey Black students who compose the top half of their high school graduating class, be admitted to Rutgers, New Brunswick.

   We demand that examinations such as the S.A.T. not be a measure of Black students admission into the college.

   We also demand that all New Jersey county college graduates be admitted automatically without further admission requirements.

   We further demand that no less than one-fifth of the total membership of the Admissions board be Black.

   We demand that these students be provided with the funds necessary for an uninterrupted educational experience.

2. *Increase of Black Faculty*

   We demand more Black teachers. Rutgers college undergraduates are not benefitting from a multiracial educational experience and we demand seven additional Black

122

teachers, forthwith, and an additional fifteen by the beginning of the first semester of 1970.

The primary source for not hiring more Black faculty is that no "qualified" Blacks are available. One reason for this is that there are in the Rutgers Graduate School over 3,000 students—40 of whom are Black—including Black foreigners. The following demands will help to alleviate this condition.

a)   Increase Black graduate school enrollment in the Fall of 1969 one-hundred percent.

b)   Give all Black second-year graduate students teaching assistantships or counsellorships as in dormitories, etc.

c)   Give junior faculty positions to all Black students who have completed their Ph.D. coursework.

d)   Recruit otherwise highly qualified personnel from the black community who may not have the conventional "academic requirements" to teach on the faculty either part-time or full time.

e)   Encourage (with fellowships and assistantships) graduating Black seniors to enter the graduate school for higher degrees.

3.   *Financial Aid for Black Students*
We demand that no less than twelve Black people (students and faculty) be appointed to the Financial Aid Board.

We further demand that the Financial Aid Office appoint a Financial Aid Officer who is Black and responsive to Black financial problems, among other duties, and who is subject to approval by the Black Unity League.

4.   *The Englehard Donation*
We recognize that the Englehard industries have made a recent donation to the university for the Graduate School of Business Administration from funds extorted from the exploitation of Black Africans.

We demand that the acceptance of this 1.25 million

dollars be based upon the condition that a substantial amount of this sum be used to set up a state-wide fund for Black students, so that the University will be purged of the argument that it is as racist as the donor's business activities have demonstrated themselves to be.

5. *Curriculum Changes*

It is in the opinion of the Black students that in order to make the university relevant and acceptable to minority groups there must be some basic changes in curriculum.

  a. We demand the institution of a four-credit course load beginning September, 1969.

  b) We demand that the first year's cumulative average for students with all remaining credits be considered as optional by these students. In the event that the student has failed a subject he will be permitted to have that subject grade erased and take a subject in place of the failed subject, if he decides to count his cumulative average. This would be retroactive for the classes of 1970 to 1972.

  c) No student should be suspended for academic reasons until after the completion of one full year of academic work.

  d) We demand, free, unhampered inter-registration between Livingston, Douglass, and Rutgers University.

6. *Restructure of the Summer Program*

It is in the opinion of the Black students that the success of the summer program depends on its complete restructure.

  a) We demand the hiring of a Black administrator to head the program. This person would be subject to the approval of the Black students.

  b) We demand the extension of the program from the two-week to a six-week period.

  c) We demand a reimbursement of a minimum of sixty dollars to compensate the students' financial loss from summer employment. This money would be additional to his financial aid packet.

d) We demand an intensified course of basic reading skills and reading comprehension.

e) We demand an intensive course in writing in relation to composition and all other courses in which a solid background in writing skills are necessary, and the continuation of the reading and writing course.

f) We demand that the setting be similar to that of a regular school day (lecture, recitation, etc.).

g) We demand the increase of Black faculty members in the program.

h) We demand the extension and modification of cultural events to Black people such as Black plays and Black experiences.

7. *Black Experience Course*

We propose that a course in "Black Experience" be instituted at Rutgers College in September, 1969. This course should be open to all students, faculty, and administration. The purpose of this is to better prepare both students, faculty, and administrators to deal with the conflicts that stem from the different life experiences of different races. This course shall be designed by Black students, faculty members, and the members of the Black community of the State of New Jersey. Full academic credit will be given to any student taking this course.

8. *Cultural Activities*

We demand that the university make known all available funds that can be used for the creation of Black Cultural programs and activities.

9. *Open Door Policy*

We demand that all social and cultural functions that are open to the entire University shall be open to the entire community.

10. *Literature of Black Contemporary Authors*

We demand a greater variety of literature of contemporary Black authors in the University Library and Book Store, as well as in the Student Centers.

11. *Employment and Wages of Minorities*
We demand an intensified program for the hiring of Black and Puerto Rican secretaries and technicians. We demand $100 a week minimum wage for all full-time employees of the University.

12. *Campus Patrol*
We will refuse to submit to improper requests made by the Campus Patrol inasmuch as they have singled out Black students and subjected us to harassment and indignities; nor will we submit to the payment of arbitrarily and illegally imposed fines.

Demands of the Black Student Unity Movement (Camden) February 10, 1969

We, the Black Student Unity Movement of Rutgers the State University, are exacting that the following demands be made operative with respect to the following date, February 17, 1969. We will not rationalize nor verbalize the non-compliance of these demands. Our demands are as follows:

1. We demand that all racist faculty be removed from the university.
2. We demand that an Urban Education Department be established.
   a. Brother Michael Edwards to be made assistant to department chairman.
      1. His job must be that of course selector, curriculum instructor, and lecturer.
   b. Establishment of an Urban Community Board
      1. Purpose—to study urban problems and make proposals for change.
   c. Degree Program
      1. B.A. or Associate Degree
3. We demand that a Black Studies Department be established.
   a. Black Students and faculty controlled.
      1. Students are to determine grading system, faculty personnel, and firing system.
      2. Financial control by students and faculty.
      3. Black Education courses
         a. African Languages
         b. Philosophy
         c. History
         d. Politics
         e. Economics

           f.   Literature

           g.   Art

           h.   Music

      4. Degree Program

           a.   B.A. or Associate Degree

4. We demand that this University hire more Black personnel other than faculty.

5. We demand that Brother Charles (Poppy) Sharp be assigned three lecture seminars.

      1. Pay should correspond to other visiting lecturers.

6. We demand that an Afro-American be made Director of Admissions for Black students.

      a. Matriculated Black students are to inform a committee to review applicants and choose director.

          1. Objective—the recruitment of 250 Black students.

          2. Establishment of a Stewart Shelton Memorial Scholarship Fund to pay tuition fees and books for each student.

7. We demand that an Afro-American be made Dean of Black Students.

8. We demand that a Black Financial Director be immediately installed.

9. We demand that a Black dormitory and recreation building be completed within the next year and a half.

10. We demand that graduate schools be established in other fields of scholarship besides Law and Education.

11. We demand that an Educational Cultural Center be established for the community and university itself.

12. We demand that the community be granted access to existing University facilities.

13. We demand that Rutgers here establish a community foundation with the initial reserve of $50,000.

14. We demand that this institution embark on an extensive program of recruiting Afro-American and Hispanic high school seniors.

15. We demand that student teaching be done within Camden City proper.
16. We demand that a Board of Academic inquiry be set up for Black students.
    a. Composition
       1. Black students and faculty
       2. Official recognition by the University
       3. Representation to be decided by the Black students.
17. We demand that classloads are to be reduced for professors.
18. We demand that a course in Racism be instituted.
    a. This course is to be taught by Brother Charles (Poppy) Sharp.
19. We demand that the existing grading system be revised so that emphasis be placed on:
    a. Field work—this is to apply in fields such as:
       1. Sociology
       2. Political Science
       3. Education
       4. Psychology
    b. Outside research—this is to be given credit.
    c. We demand that course requirements be revised in order to allot more time to field experience.
20. We demand a pay increase for professors and non-professionals
21. We demand that the new library addition be named after Brother Paul Robeson. Livingston College to be renamed Robeson University.
22. We demand that college credit be granted for black life experience.
    ex. Waive certain irrelevant courses.
23. We demand that a night preparatory division be set up to accommodate high school drop-outs and any interested persons.
24. We demand that a Black section be set aside in the now

existing University Library and name it after Dr. Ulysses Wiggins.
a. Composition
    1. Books
    2. Filmstrips
    3. Records
    4. Tapes
    5. Periodicals

Appendix VI

Resolution of the Board of Governors of Rutgers University, March 14, 1969

The University, as part of a state-wide system of higher education which in addition to the different divisions of the University also includes the state colleges and community colleges, pledges itself to work with these other institutions to the end that every holder of a New Jersey secondary school diploma may find that form of higher education which is best suited to his needs, abilities, and aspirations.

However, the Board recognizes that such a program is not now available. Therefore, the Board agrees to establish a new and pioneering program by September, 1969, which initially will open college doors to educationally and economically disadvantaged graduates of secondary schools in those communities where Rutgers has its primary locations and its most significant community obligations—Newark, New Brunswick, and Camden. The objective of this program is to make it possible for those graduates to achieve a true Rutgers degree. As this new program succeeds, and as additional funds become available, the University, together with the other institutions, will expand the program to the full objective stated in the first paragraph above.

The University will seek additional funds from the State Legislature to initiate the new program by September, 1969. If these are not available, the University will fund the program from other sources to insure that it will become a reality in the next academic year.

Notes

One. Introduction

1. Although there is a vast and growing literature on the student
movements of the 1960s, there is as yet no comprehensive study
of the black student protests that emerged on predominantly
white campuses after 1965. There was a rash of books and articles dealing with the subject between 1968 and 1973, including
Earl Anthony, *The Time of Furnaces: A Case Study of Black Student Revolt* (New York, 1971); William Barlow and Peter Sha-
piro, *The End to Silence: The San Francisco State College Student
Movement in the '60s* (New York, 1971); James McEvoy and
Abraham Miller, eds., *Black Power and Student Rebellion* (Bel-
mont, Mass., 1969); Cushing Strout and David Grossnagel,
eds., *Divided We Stand: Reflections on the Crisis at Cornell* (New
York, 1971); and Charles V. Willie and Arline S. McCord, *Black
Students at White Colleges* (New York, 1972). The best of the
contemporary accounts is Julian Foster and Durward Long,
eds., *Protest* (New York, 1970), especially Long's chapter, "Black

133

Protest." Marvin W. Peterson et al., *Black Students on White Campuses: The Impacts of Increased Black Enrollments* (Ann Arbor, 1978) examines in some depth the experiences of thirteen colleges and universities. William H. Exum's *Paradoxes of Protest: Black Student Activism in a White University* (Philadelphia, 1985) stands virtually alone as a sophisticated case study of a single institution, New York University.

2. The Civil Rights Act of 1964 required colleges and universities to report data on racial identities, but because most institutions did not maintain such records, they were slow in complying. In 1967 Rutgers University sought to meet the federal mandate by distributing questionnaires to students, but many (40 percent) failed to return them. A year later, students were asked to state their racial identity during the registration process. Thus reliable figures on the racial composition of the student body are not available prior to 1968. *Caellian,* October 6, 1967; January 26, 1968. (*Caellian* was the student newspaper at Douglass College.) For the national estimates of black enrollment, see the excellent survey by John Egerton, *State Universities and Black Americans: An Inquiry into Desegregation and Equity for Negroes in 100 Public Universities* (Atlanta, 1969). Egerton estimated that in the academic year, 1967–1968, only about 2 percent of those enrolled in predominantly white colleges and universities were black, and that half of those were first-year students.

3. For background, see Richard P. McCormick, *Rutgers: A Bicentennial History* (New Brunswick, 1966) and the author's "Rutgers, the State University," in David Riesman and Verne A. Stadtman, eds., *Academic Transformation: Seventeen Institutions under Pressure* (New York, 1973).

Two. Stirrings of Change

1. The Harris case is well covered by Terry Perlin, "The Ordeal of Don Harris," *Rutgers Alumni Monthly,* November 1963, pp. 7–8, 17; *Targum* (Rutgers College student newspaper), September–December 1963; and the *Newark Evening News,* September 27, 1963.

  Harris was subsequently on the staff of the Select Committee on Equal Educational Opportunity of the U.S. Senate and chief of staff to Mayor Kenneth A. Gibson of Newark. He joined Philip Morris Incorporated in 1978 and became director of communications, Philip Morris International, in 1985.

2. *Rutgers Newsletter,* May 1965; *Targum,* December 12, 1963; January 1, 9, 1964; May 14, 1964.
3. *Rutgers Newsletter,* May 1965.
4. Papers of President Mason W. Gross, box 23, DHE-EOF (hereafter cited as Papers MWG). Unless otherwise indicated, all manuscript sources may be found in the Department of Special Collections, Alexander Library, Rutgers, the State University.
5. Herbert R. Kells, *Unfinished Business: Equal Opportunity at Rutgers-1968* (New Brunswick, 1968), *passim;* Egerton, *State Universities,* p. 37; *Rutgers Newsletter,* May 24, 1968.
6. Papers MWG, box 9, Equal Opportunity Program.
7. *Rutgers Newsletter,* May 24, 1968.
8. Interview with Jerome C. Harris, Jr., November 22, 1988.
   Harris received a master's degree in urban planning from Rutgers, held senior positions in the Department of Higher Education, and is now vice-president for governmental affairs of the Greater Newark Chamber of Commerce.
9. Interview with Karen Predow-James, November 11, 1988.
   Predow-James earned a doctorate in sociology at Rutgers and is currently a vice-president of Citibank, New York.
10. Interview with Richard W. Roper, November 29, 1988.
    Roper is assistant dean for governmental affairs at the Woodrow Wilson School of Public and International Affairs, Princeton University.
11. Harris interview; *Caellian,* April 28, 1967. According to one source, the Student Afro-American Society was first organized at Columbia University by Hilton Clark, son of the noted psychologist, Dr. Kenneth Clark, in 1965. Jerry L. Avron, *University in Revolt: A History of the Columbia Crisis* (London, 1969), pp. 20–21.
12. *Caellian,* March 14, 1968; Predow-James interview.
13. *Caellian,* January 26, March 8, 1968.
14. *Caellian* in this period was far more sensitive to racial concerns than *Targum* and reported extensively on events relevant to blacks.

Three. A New Urgency

1. Interview with Leon Green, December 12, 1988.
   Green received his doctorate from the Rutgers Graduate School of Applied and Professional Psychology and is a staff psychologist at East Orange Veterans Hospital in New Jersey.
2. *Caellian*, April 5, 1968.
3. Ibid., April 12, 1968; *Targum*, April 8, 1968.
4. *Targum*, April 8–16, 1968; *Caellian*, April 12, 1968.
5. *Targum*, April 10, 1968; *Rutgers Newsletter*, April 26, 1968; *Rutgers Alumni Monthly*, May 1968, pp. 11–12.
6. *Caellian*, April 12, 1968.
7. Ibid., April 12, 19, May 3, September 13, 1968; *Targum*, April 26, 1968.
8. *Targum*, April 10, 1968.
9. Ibid., April 10, 15, 1968.
10. Minutes, Board of Governors, April 11, 1968; *Caellian*, April 12, 1968.
11. Interview with Vicki Donaldson, November 29, 1988.
    Donaldson obtained a degree from the Rutgers Law School in Newark, served on the Newark Board of Education, and has a private law practice in East Orange.
12. Minutes, Special Meeting, Board of Governors, April 19, 1968; *Rutgers Newsletter*, April 26, 1968; *Caellian*, April 26, 1968; Harris, Predow-James, Roper, and Donaldson interivews. For the fourteen demands presented to the Board, see Appendix I.
13. Minutes, Board of Governors, May 10, 1968. The board was informed that between 1953 and 1967 only 214 blacks had received baccalaureate degrees from all divisions of the University and that there were 67 blacks among the 3,808 "academic professionals" at Rutgers. Apparently the term "academic professionals" included not only regular faculty but numerous administrative categories as well. In actuality there were fifteen faculty members in May 1968, six of them at Rutgers College.
14. *Rutgers Newsletter*, May 24, 1968.
15. Dean Willard Heckel to Gross, April 12, 1968, Papers MWG, box 4, Blacks; *Rutgers Newsletter*, February 28, 1969.
16. John R. Martin to Dean Milton Schwebel, July 10, 1968, Papers of Provost Richard Schlatter, box 52. Among the visiting lectur-

ers was the Rev. Dr. Samuel D. Proctor, who received permanent appointment as Martin Luther King Professor in 1969. On
John R. Martin, see *Faculty Newsletter*, May 24, 1968.

17. Kells, *Unfinished Business, passim*; Egerton, *State Universities*, pp.
37–40. The early programs to aid minority students focused
almost exclusively on blacks, but in October 1968, the Douglass
College Equal Opportunity Committee made plans to include
Puerto Ricans in their recruitment efforts. It was estimated that
there were then five Puerto Rican women at the college.
Caellian, October 25, 1968.

18. *Rutgers Newsletter*, April 12, 1968.

Four. The Breaking Point

1. A useful account of the protest movement in Newark is David J.
Samuels, "Anatomy of a Takeover: The Black Organization of
Students at Rutgers University in Newark" written in 1986 as an
undergraduate paper at Harvard University. Irwin L. Merker et
al., "A Report about the Faculty of the Newark College of Arts
and Sciences, the Recruitment and Education of Disadvantaged
Students, and the February–March Disturbances at the Newark
Campus," June 1969 (cited hereafter as Merker Report), re-
counts the story from the faculty's perspective. The document
was prepared in response to charges made against the faculty by
Chancellor Ralph A. Dungan. Also relevant is a chronology of
events at the Newark campus from February 6, 1968 to March
6, 1969, prepared by Malcolm Talbott, vice-president for Newark. Papers MWG, box 7, Disruptions-Newark. Most of the key
documents were brought together by James Ramsay, Newark-
Rutgers associate provost, and have been retained by him in his
office.

2. The Board of Governors met in Newark November 22, 1968,
and heard presentations by students, faculty, and administrators
in support of their request for a larger share of the funds. Minutes of the Board of Governors, November 22, 1968; *Rutgers
Observer* (the student newspaper in Newark), November 20,
1968.

3. Interviews with Robert Curvin, December 5, 1988; James H.
Ramsay, November 29, 1988; Gustav Heningburg, November

29, 1988; Vicki Donaldson, November 29, 1988; Richard Roper, November 29, 1988.

Curvin received his doctorate in Political Science from Princeton, taught at Brooklyn College and the New School for Social Research, and served on the editorial board of the *New York Times.* He is now a vice-president of the Ford Foundation.

Ramsay left his teaching position at Cedar Grove High School in 1969 to join the Urban University Department at Rutgers-Newark. A year later he became the chair of that department. He has also served as mayor of Montclair, New Jersey.

4. Samuels, "Anatomy of a Takeover," pp. 5–6; *Rutgers Observer,* October 31, November 12, 1968.

5. Donaldson interview.

6. Curvin interview.

7. Harrison Snell to Board of Governors [April 1968], Papers MWG, box 4, Blacks. For these demands, see Appendix II.

8. Merker Report, *passim;* Minutes, Newark College of Arts and Sciences [NCAS] Faculty, October 17, 1968.

9. *Rutgers Observer,* October 31, 1968.

10. Samuels, "Anatomy of a Takeover," pp. 9–10. For these demands, see Appendix III.

11. Talbott Chronology, Papers MWG, box 7, Disruptions-Newark.

12. Donaldson and Curvin interviews; *Newark Evening News,* February 24, 25, 1969; *Rutgers Observer,* February 26–28, 1969.

13. Donaldson interview; *Rutgers Observer,* February 26–28, 1969.

14. President Gross received hundreds of letters and telegrams critical of his leniency toward the protesters, many of them citing Father Hesburgh's statement. Papers MWG, box 7, Disruptions-Newark.

15. Interviews with Curvin, Heningburg, and Roper.

16. A substantial portion of these negotiations was tape recorded, and there is a twenty-eight-page, single-spaced transcript, "Special Meeting with Administrators and B.O.S. Representatives" in Papers MWG, box 7, Disruptions-Newark.

17. For the demands presented by BOS on February 6, 1969, see Appendix III. In the course of the subsequent negotiations, these demands went through four revisions. A collation of the five versions can be found in Papers, MWG, box 7, Disruptions-Newark, together with the responses made by the University negotiators. It runs to forty-seven single-spaced typed pages. See also *Rutgers Observer,* February 26, 28, March 5, 1969. No

"signed agreement" can be located in the University Archives. The document in question was rushed down to Gross at his residence early on the morning of February 27 for his signature. He later told a legislative committee: "I signed no agreement as such. I have to admit that there was some misunderstanding, but the one agreement that I was supposed to have signed was one that I tried to persuade the students all along could not be signed. . . . The matter was a matter for the faculty." On the evacuation of Conklin Hall, see *Newark Evening News,* February 27, 1969; *Rutgers Observer,* February 28, 1969.

18. Some of the subsequent difficulties arose from the fact that Joe Browne, who had succeeded Harrison Snell as the head of BOS, stated to a meeting of the NCAS student body on February 27 that the administration was committed to admit black Newark high school graduates who ranked in the top half of their class, or who had verbal SAT scores of 400 or more. See the Merker Report, Appendix I, which is a detailed narrative of the negotiations on the admissions issue down to March 14, 1969.

19. Ibid. Talbott reported to the NCAS faculty shortly after noon on February 27 on the negotiations with BOS. He had only five hours sleep in the previous four days and had to cut short his narrative because of exhaustion. Two members of BOS also addressed the faculty meeting. Minutes, NCAS Faculty, February 27, 1969. Talbott next met with the faculty on March 3, when his efforts to defend his negotiations with BOS brought forth hostile reactions. Minutes, NCAS Faculty, March 3, 1969.

20. Minutes, NCAS Faculty, March 6, 1969.

21. Ibid.

22. *Rutgers Observer,* March 12, 1969.

23. Ibid., March 19, 1969. On March 14, Professor Henry Blumenthal, a highly respected member of the faculty, was appointed dean of NCAS, replacing Talbott, who had been serving as acting dean.

24. *Rutgers Observer,* March 19, 1969. There were last-minute efforts on March 13 to resolve the admissions impasse. Chancellor Dungan came to Newark, where he met with members of the NCAS Student Council and the Joint Scholastic Standing–Admissions Committee. Later that evening he talked with representatives of BOS, who had refused to meet with the other groups. On the morning of March 14, the associate dean sum-

139

moned the officers of BOS to meet with appropriate faculty committees and administrative officers. Bos declined, stating that the time for talking had passed; what they wanted now was action. The relevant documents are in James Ramsay's files.

25. Kells, *Unfinished Business;* L. C. Doak to S. Plehn, November 22, 1968, Papers MWG, box 9, Equal Opportunity Programs; Egerton, *State Universities.* pp. 36–48. In October 1968, the Executive Committee of the Rutgers Alumni Association appointed an ad hoc committee that raised questions critical of the University's programs for disadvantaged students. Herbert R. Kells in his response pointed to the small numbers of such students but said that more would be coming in the future. Kells to Vincent Kramer, November 18, 1968, Papers MWG, box 37, UUP.

26. Interview, Leon Green, December 12, 1988.

27. Harris interview.

28. Green interview.

29. Harris interview.

30. Harris to Earle Clifford [no date], Papers MWG, box 7, Disruptions-New Brunswick.

31. Rutgers College SAS to Dean Arnold B. Grobman, February 12, 1969, Papers MWG, box 7, Disruptions-New Brunswick; *Targum,* February 13–24, 1969. Grobman had expressed his doubts about black studies courses taught and taken exclusively by blacks on the grounds that they encouraged separation, rather than pluralism. *Rutgers Newsletter,* December 20, 1968.

32. *Targum,* February 26, 1969; *Caellian,* February 21, 28, 1969.

33. *Targum,* February 27, 1969.

34. Ibid., February 28, March 3, 4, 1969. For the text of Randy Green's speech, see *Targum,* special supplement, May 24, 1969.

35. Ibid., March 3, 1969.

36. "Report on Current Status of Items of Interest to Black Students in the College," February 28, 1969, Papers MWG, box 7, Disruptions-New Brunswick; *Targum,* March 4, 1969.

37. *Targum,* March 5, 1969. The demands can be found in Appendix IV.

38. On the work of the Select Committee, see Papers, Richard P. McCormick, box 15, Select Committee. While this committee was meeting, Wright and representatives of the black students conferred with top administrative officials to reach agreement on issues that were beyond the scope of the college faculty. *Targum,*

special supplement, May 24, 1969. The faculty's resolutions are recorded in its minutes and in *Rutgers Newsletter,* March 14, 1969.

39. Papers, R. P. McCormick, box 15, Special Committee.
40. Minutes, Rutgers College Faculty, May 28, 1969; Papers, R. P. McCormick, box 15, Correspondence; *Rutgers Newsletter.* April 4, 1969.
41. Testimony of Dean Margery Foster, "Public Hearing before Senate and Assembly Committees on Education," June 9, 1969 (mimeo, 1969), pp. 154A–157A; *Caellian,* October 18, 25, 1968.
42. Predow-James interview; *Caellian,* October 25, 1969.
43. Ibid., February 21, 1969.
44. Ibid., February 28, 1969.
45. Ibid.
46. Ibid.
47. Ibid., March 14, 1969; Minutes, Douglass College Faculty, March 11, 1969.
48. *Caellian,* October 17, 1969, gives the full text of this lengthy report. There were eighty-one black students in the new entering class, together with twenty-two UUD students. A six-week summer program enrolled forty-one specially admitted women. The college now had eleven black faculty, four of whom were full-time. There was an African and African-American House in operation, as well as the rudiments of a Black Studies program.
49. Ibid., March 14, 1969.
50. There is a useful "Chronology and Background" attached to Ralph A. Dungan, "A Report to the New Jersey Legislature Concerning the Recent Events and Disturbances at the Newark and Camden Campuses of Rutgers, the State University" (mimeo, March 31, 1969), pp. 14–15. See also "Public Hearing," testimony of Dean Layton Hall.
51. The demands can be found in Appendix V.
52. *Camden Courier-Post,* February 27, 1969; *Rutgers Newsletter,* March 14, 1969.
53. *Camden Courier-Post,* February 28, 1969, reported that twenty-five individuals, including two infants, occupied the building, and that only nine were students at CSJ. Among the students who were identified were Roy Jones, Thomas Warren, and Aaron Thompson. The others were community activists associated

with BPUM, including that organization's co-chairman, Michael Edwards, who held an appointment as "resource assistant" in the Sociology Department.

54. For the text of Gross's letter, see *Rutgers Newsletter,* March 14, 1969.

55. *Camden Courier-Post,* March 3–5, 1969. In an editorial on February 28, the *Courier-Post* strongly condemned the "forcible seizure" of the College Center, called on the civil authorities to prosecute the lawbreakers, and urged President Gross to take a hard line. The CSJ student paper, *The Gleaner,* was supportive of the BSUM and critical of the *Courier-Post* editorial.

56. Dean of the College to Faculty and Students, March 17, 1969, Papers MWG, box 7, Disruptions-South Jersey. Gross addressed the CSJ faculty on March 6 to tell them that while Camden would get its "fair share" of the University budget, there would not be much additional funding for the new programs that the BSUM had demanded. *Camden Courier-Post,* March 7, 1969.

Five. *"A New and Pioneering Program"*

1. Minutes of the Board of Governors, Executive Session, March 14, 1969; interview with Charles A. Jurgensen, January 4, 1989; Jurgensen to R. P. McCormick, December 9, 1988; Heningburg interview.

2. For the origins of this statement, see Merker Report, Appendix I.

3. For the full text of the document, see Appendix VI. This "new and pioneering program" was not the product of any prior discussions; it was wholly concocted during the Executive Session. See testimony of President Gross in "Public Hearing," pp. 54–55.

4. *Newark Evening News,* March 5, 1969.

5. Papers MWG, box 37, UUP, contains this voluminous correspondence, as well as the resolutions adopted by the Rutgers Alumni Association.

6. Dungan, "Report to the New Jersey Legislature." That the main concern of the legislature was with the "disturbances," rather than with the issue of expanding access to the University, is evident from the fact that the "Report" dealt only with Newark

and Camden; the protests in New Brunswick were all but ignored. On the bills to penalize students involved in campus "disorders," see *Rutgers Newsletter,* May 2, 1969.

7. Gross to Sen. W. T. Hiering and Assemb. Thomas H. Kean, May 1, 1969, Papers MWG, box 7, Disruptions, 1969, Legislature.

8. "Public Hearing,"; George Holsten to Gross, June 25, 1969, Papers MWG, box 37, UUP. The transcript of the hearing reveals the numerous reservations the legislators had about the program.

9. Minutes, Board of Trustees, June 6, 1969; Minutes, Board of Governors, June 13, 1969. The preambles to both resolutions cited the approval given by the State Board of Higher Education to the Rutgers programs and its pledge to support the University's application to the legislature for supplemental funds. The boards anticipated that the legislature would act favorably in the near future. On the action taken by the State Board of Higher Education, see its memorandum of March 21, 1969, to Presidents and Trustees, New Jersey Public Institutions of Higher Education, Papers MWG, box 37, UUP.

10. The Urban University Program is fully described in two documents of April 30 and May 15, 1969. These, and other relevant materials are in Papers, MWG, box 37, UUP. There is considerable documentation on the operation of the Urban University Program in New Brunswick in the Papers of Elinor Ross, the director of the program, especially box 3. See also *Rutgers Newsletter,* May 2, 30, September 16, 1969.

11. Papers, Elinor Ross, box 3.

12. Ibid.; *Rutgers Newsletter,* September 16, 1969.

13. Nancy Winterbauer, "An Analysis of the 1968–1969 Black Student Disturbances at Rutgers University" (Ed.D. dissertation, Rutgers, 1980), is a useful study of the Urban University Program.

14. Ramsay interview; Curvin interview; William W. Wiles to Dean Henry Blumenthal, February 25, 1970, Papers, Elinor Ross, box 3.

15. Report by Associate Dean Warren Manspeizer, NCAS, April 6, 1971, Papers, Elinor Ross, box 3.

16. Elinor Ross to Blenda J. Wilson, March 24, 1970; Charles V. Longo to Dean Arnold B. Grobman, Rutgers College, October 13, 1969; Report, "The Urban University Program," prepared

by Mary D. Howard, March 1970, Papers, Elinor Ross, box 3.
For a different appraisal, see *Rutgers Newsletter,* October 20,
1970.

17. Allen D. Ballard, Jr., "Report on Urban University Program at
the New Brunswick Campus," Papers, Elinor Ross, box 3.

18. *Livingston Medium,* February 18, 1971.

Six. *The Educational Opportunity Fund*

1. "An Interim Report Covering the First Term of Operation of the
Educational Opportunity Fund" (State Department of Higher
Education, mimeo, June 13, 1969); *The Chancellor's Report,
1967–1969* (State Department of Higher Education, 1969), pp.
9–10; Dungan to Gross, November 10, 1967. Papers MWG, box
23, DHE-EOF.

3. Chapter 142, *Laws of New Jersey, 1968.*

3. "Interim Report," *passim.*

4. Gross to Dungan, January 5, June 21, 1968, Papers MWG, box
23, DHE-EOF. On July 25, Dungan informed Gross in a telegram
that Rutgers' participation in the Educational Opportunity
Fund program had been approved.

5. *Chancellor's Report, 1967–1969,* Appendix H. By contrast, Essex
County College, a two-year institution, received 531 slots. Rutgers did succeed in persuading the Department of Higher Education that up to 10 percent of EOF slots should be available for
graduate students. H. R. Kells to R. A. Rettig, October 10,
1968; Dungan to New Jersey Colleges and Universities, January
22, 1969, Papers MWG, box 23, DHE-EOF. For the first semester,
1969–1970, Rutgers was allotted 613 slots.

6. John R. Martin to Dean Arnold B. Grobman, May 26, 1969;
Blenda J. Wilson to R. Schlatter, E. Young, and J. R. Martin,
July 15, 1969; Arthur Richmond to Dungan, July 30, 1969,
Papers, Elinor Ross, box 3.

7. John R. Martin to Gross, November 14, 1969; Gross to
Dungan, November 20, 1969, Papers MWG, box 37, UUP;
Blenda J. Wilson to William Kolodinsky, March 30, 1970, Pa-
pers, Richard Schlatter, box 49, UUP. Wilson, who had joined
Provost Schlatter's staff in May 1969, was designated university

coordinator of the UUP and TYP programs in April 1970. *Rutgers Newsletter,* October 27, 1972.

8. L. H. Ruppert to Sen. R. H. Bateman, January 5, 1970, Papers, Elinor Ross, box 3; *Rutgers Newsletter,* January 30, 1970.

9. *Rutgers Newsletter,* March 3, April 24, May 8, 1970. Chancellor Dungan and the State Board of Higher Education supported the University's request for the supplemental appropriation, but the quid pro quo was the incorporation of the funds in the EOF budget.

10. Chapter 174, *Laws of New Jersey, 1970; Rutgers Newsletter,* April 24, 1970.

11. Blenda J. Wilson to Juanita High, April 21, 1970; Dungan to H. R. Winkler, April 17, 1970, Papers, Richard Schlatter, box 49, UUP.

12. Schlatter to Deans Blumenthal, Foster, Grobman, Lynton, and Young, December 16, 1970, Papers, Richard Schlatter, box 49, UUP.

13. Dungan to Schlatter, March 30, 1971; Schlatter to Dungan, April 20, 1971, Papers, Richard Schlatter, box 49, UUP.

14. Solomon Arbeiter, Assistant Chancellor, to Schlatter, April 20, 1971, Papers, Richard Schlatter, box 49, UUP.

15. Arbeiter to Schlatter, June 25, 1971; Schlatter to Arbeiter, July 14, 1971, Papers MWG, box 23, DHE-EOF; *Rutger's Newsletter,* October 11, 1971; Minutes, Ad Hoc Committee on Special Programs for Disadvantaged Students, April–May 1971, Papers MWG, box 4, Blacks.

16. This Ad Hoc Committee on Special Programs, chaired by Dean Milton Schwebel of the Graduate School of Education, met from May 25, 1971, to May 28, 1972. For the minutes of the committee and its report, see Papers, Elinor Ross, box 3. The key recommendation was that each college should establish an Academic Foundations department "to support the academic matriculation and personal adjustment of educationally disadvantaged students." Representatives of Rutgers and Douglass signed a statement to the effect that their colleges would be free to provide such services in ways differing from that delineated in the report.

17. See, for example, Juanita High, Executive Director, EOF, to B. J. Wilson, June 8, 1972; High to EOF Board of Directors, February 20, 1974, Papers, Elinor Ross, box 3.

Seven. Postscript

1. The data cited here, and elsewhere throughout this chapter, are taken from the voluminous and detailed reports prepared by the Office of Institutional Studies and by the Office of Assistant Vice-President for Academic Affairs–Retention. Prior to 1973, record keeping was not well organized, but starting with that year increasingly useful reports could be generated from reliable data bases.

2. McCormick, "Rutgers, the State University," pp. 281–282; *Rutgers Newsletter,* April 12, 26, August 3, 1971.

3. For reasons mentioned in the Preface, this book is focused on protests by African American students. It has not dealt with the efforts of other minority groups, notably Puerto Ricans, to secure recognition and access. Down to 1969 there were few Puerto Rican students at Rutgers. In November 1968, President Gross had met with representatives of the Comité Pro-Educacion Profesional del Puertoriqueño and agreed to add Puerto Rican recruiters to the admissions staffs in Newark and New Brunswick. In March 1969, a newly formed student group at Newark, the Puerto Rican Organization, presented demands to Acting Dean Talbott that called for stepped-up recruiting efforts, remedial programs, and the appointment of Puerto Ricans to the faculty. Puerto Rican students were early participants in the EOF and Urban University programs. In October 1969, the Douglass College Equal Opportunity Board set up a special committee to recruit Puerto Rican students. Livingston College introduced a program in Puerto Rican studies. The first organized protest by Puerto Rican students occurred at Camden on March 1, 1971, when a group occupied the dean's office for two hours and demanded a meeting with top officials in New Brunswick. A few days later, thirty students representing all five undergraduate day colleges met with Acting President Schlatter. They wanted more Puerto Rican recruiters, financial aid administrators, and faculty. They soon received a fourteen-page response by the vice-president of student affairs that explained what was being done to meet their demands. By 1974, there were 433 Puerto Rican full-time undergraduates; that figure rose slowly to 770 by 1988,

146

when "other Hispanics" numbered 1,115. Minutes, Board of Governors, November 8, 1968; Puerto Rican Organization to Talbott, March 10, 1969, Papers MWG, box 7, Disruptions-Newark; *Caellian,* October 24, 1969; *Rutgers Newsletter,* March 15, 29, 1971.

4. What follows is not intended to be a complete catalogue of the protests, useful as such an account might be. In general, I have confined this narrative to protests that involved more than one college or that elicited responses from the central administration.

5. *Rutgers Newsletter,* April 12, 26, 1971.

6. Ibid., March 29, 1971.

7. Michael Rockland, *Report of the Commission on Ethnic and Race Relations of Douglass College* (New Brunswick, 1972); *Rutgers Newsletter,* February 7, 1972.

8. *Rutgers Newsletter,* November 9, 1973. Dr. Edward J. Bloustein succeeded Mason W. Gross as president of Rutgers in 1971 and served until his death on December 9, 1989.

9. Ibid., November 16, December 13, 1973.

10. "Promises to Keep," Papers, Edward J. Bloustein, box 7, f. 17.

11. *Targum,* April 13, 1979.

12. Winterbauer, "Black Student Disturbances," Table 7.

13. *Rutgers Newsletter,* April 20, 1979; *Targum,* April 20, 1979.

14. Minutes, Board of Governors, May 11, 1979.

15. *Special Report: University Response to Minority Concerns,* September 4, 1979; Minutes, Board of Governors, September 14, 1979. President Bloustein devoted his commencement address in June to the recent protest. Excerpts of his remarks were published in the *New York Times,* July 22, 1979.

16. *Targum,* February 25, March 3, 1980; *Rutgers Newsletter,* March 7, 28, 1980; Minutes, Board of Governors, March 14, 1980.

17. *1980 Report on Minority Concerns: The Rutgers Campus at New Brunswick,* September 2, 1980: *Rutgers Newsletter,* September 5, 1980.

18. The principal source of these data is Chancellor T. Edward Hollander's Memorandum of March 14, 1986, to Members, Board of Higher Education, on the subject: Policy Initiatives to Address Declining Minority Enrollment, copy in author's files.

19. See note 18.

20. Minutes, Board of Governors, April 11, 1986.

21. For a full report on the "Challenge '69" project, including recommendations for future initiatives, see "Answering the Challenge," submitted to President Bloustein, October 1989.
22. There are succinct analyses of declining black enrollments nation wide in *One-Third of a Nation: A Report of the Commission on Minority Participation in Education and American Life* (Washington, D.C. 1988).
23. Data presented to the Board of Governors Ad Hoc Committee on Minority Recruitment and Retention, November 23, 1988.
24. *Report on Minority Affairs, Fall, 1989,* a publication of the Office of the Senior Vice-President for Academic Affairs. This report is a comprehensive summary of minority-oriented programs as of 1989.

Index

Printed in the United States
64924LVS00002B/28